BEGINNING DIVING

Marian Barone
Temple University

National Press Books

Dedicated to my mother

Copyright © 1973 by Marian Barone
First edition 1973

All rights reserved. No portion of this book may be reproduced in any form or by any means without written permission of the publisher.

Library of Congress Catalog Card Number: 72-97845
International Standard Book Numbers: 0-87484-252-2 (paper)
0-87484-253-0 (cloth)

Manufactured in the United States of America

National Press Books
850 Hansen Way, Palo Alto, California 94304

This book was set in Helvetica by Typographic Service Company and was printed and bound by Kingsport Press. The drawings were done by Jenny Barone and Gerald Gabow, and the cover photograph was taken by Dick Keeble. The designer of both text and cover was Nancy Sears, and the text layout was done by Mary Wiley. Sponsoring editor was Richard W. Bare, and Michelle Hogan supervised production.

CONTENTS

FOREWORD vii

PREFACE ix

1 EQUIPMENT 1

The Diving Area 1
The Bottom 2
The Springboard 2
The Fulcrum 3

2 THE FUNDAMENTALS OF DIVING 5

The Ability to Swim 5
Exhaling in the Water 6
A Front Dive from the Side of the Pool 6
Body Positions in Diving 7
Fundamental Exercises for Diving 8
The Approach Forward 12
The Approach Backward 20
The Entry 24

3 THE CATEGORIES OF DIVES   28

    The Forward Category   28
    The Backward Category   29
    The Reverse Category   29
    The Inward Category   30
    The Twisting Category   30
    Fundamental to Advanced Dives   31

4 WHERE TO BEGIN—ONE METER   35

    Beginning Dives, One Meter:
    Required List   36

1. Forward Dive, Straight Position   36
2. Back Dive, Straight Position   40
3. Forward Dive, One-Half Twist, Straight Position   44
3a. Forward Dive, Pike Position   48
4. Inward Dive, Pike Position   52
4a. Inward Dive, Straight Position   55
5. Reverse Dive, Straight Position   56

    Intermediate Dives, One Meter:
    Optional List   59

6. Forward Dive, One Somersault, Tuck Position   59
7. Back Dive, One Somersault, Tuck Position   63
8. Forward Dive, One and One-Half Somersault, Tuck Position   65
8a. Forward Dive, One and One-Half Somersault, Pike Position   68
9. Inward Dive, One Somersault, Tuck Position   68
10. Reverse Dive, One Somersault, Tuck Position   72
11. Forward Dive, One and One-Half Somersault, One-Half Twist, Tuck Position   75

5 WHERE TO BEGIN—THREE METER   78

    Beginning Dives, Three Meter   79

1. Falling Forward Dive, Straight Position   79
2. Falling Back Dive, Straight Position   79

Completing the List, Three Meter 80
Dry Land Practice 81

6 OTHER AIDS IN LEARNING TO DIVE   82

Trampoline 82
Films and Tapes 83
Jackets 84
Practice Sessions 84
A Good Beginning List for
   Competition 85
What the Judges Look for in a
   Good Dive 86
Diving Sheet 90

FOREWORD

Graceful as a cat strides the diver down the board, converting his energy into an explosive hurdle, catapulting into the air, and knifing smoothly into the calm water. The spectacle of springboard diving, either at the local pool or at the Olympic Games, never ceases to amaze and delight us all.

Marian Barone has prepared this book for all who want to dive themselves or coach others. The detailed explanations and coaching points, coupled with clear illustrations, should enable the beginner to develop his confidence and both the novice and advanced diver to analyze their performance for improvement. Coaches and teachers can benefit from her comments and teaching progressions as well.

I have watched Miss Barone work with young men and women for several years and admire not only her skill at analyzing movements and the clarity of her communication with students, but also her ability to motivate them, her love of the activity, and her humor. An all-around athlete herself, she not only was a nationally ranked diver, but also holds a national record in track and field and in the 1948 Olympics won the bronze medal in Gymnastics: the last American woman to have done so. Currently she is on the physical education faculty at Temple University, where she teaches and coaches Women's Gymnastics and Diving.

Probably the greatest vote of confidence one can give a teacher is to ask that she work with one's own children. I have already given that vote, for she has coached my own son, whose films were used as the basis for the illustrations in this book. His selection to the All-Eastern prep school team must be attributed to a great degree to the skill and patience of Marian Barone. I am sure you will find these same qualities in the pages of her book.

I feel it rates a perfect "10"!

> Thomas Evaul
> Coordinator, Physical Education
> Temple University

PREFACE

It is my firm belief that diving from the springboard cannot be learned alone, either by practice or by reviewing books and films. These factors are, of course, essential in learning to dive, but the *heart* of the process is the constant on-the-spot interaction between diver and teacher or coach. Two divers may also accomplish this interaction by assuming these roles alternately in practice.

This book is designed, therefore, not only for the beginning diver but also for the second person who will observe the dive. It may be considered an explanation of both the fundamentals of *diving* and the fundamentals of *teaching diving*. The principles of board work and diving presented here may be used to teach a youngster to dive merely for the pleasure of it or to introduce the student to competitive diving.

Marian Barone

EQUIPMENT

Every sport involves certain calculated risks. The equipment used for that sport, however, can greatly reduce the risk. Diving is no exception: personal injury can result from faulty or inadequate equipment as much as from inexperience or poor judgment. Even though beginning divers seem to worry most about a flat entry (or "slap") into the water, that usually results in little more than a sting or embarrassment. The real danger lies in hitting the bottom with great force, slipping on the board, or hitting the board after take-off. Beginning divers should be aware of the real danger and learn to laugh at an occasional flat entry.

THE DIVING AREA

The diving area or diving well may vary according to the age of the original pool and diving board installation, but certain standards are necessary for the safety of the diver.

For one-meter and three-meter diving boards, there should be at least twenty feet of unobstructed deep water extending out from the tip of the boards, and at least seven feet of unobstructed deep water on each side of the boards.

THE BOTTOM

For the one-meter board, the bottom of the pool should be at least ten (and preferably twelve) feet deep. The minimum bottom depth for the three-meter board is twelve feet (and preferably fourteen feet). Good diving requires that the body go through the water fully extended and tensed in the vertical position. An adult going through the water in this position will reach the bottom of as much as fifteen feet of water with considerable speed.

The bottom should be flat. Pool bottoms that curve upwards towards shallow water are dangerous in the diving area. The bottom should be free of all obstructions such as rough concrete, drains, and dark areas. The water must be clear enough for the diver to see the bottom.

THE SPRINGBOARD

Most modern boards are sixteen feet in length, to give ample room for the diver's steps and hurdle to the end of the board. The sixteen-foot board also allows maximum variation in fulcrum setting. The sixteen-foot board is required for all college and Amateur Athletic Union championship diving competitions. A board that is shorter than sixteen feet will require adjustments by the diver in the number of steps taken to the end of the board and adjustments in lift-off speed from the board.

The majority of pool equipment suppliers are manufacturing boards of aluminum or fiberglass with a rough surface finish. Such boards greatly minimize the danger of slipping and they are extremely durable and consistent in response.

THE FULCRUM

The fulcrum, or standard on which the board rests, is usually placed one-third of the distance from the back end of the board. Modern fiberglass boards and fulcrum installations include a wheel which may adjust the angle of the board upward or downward at its tip or forward end. When the fulcrum wheel is moved forward, the tip of the board rises approximately two inches, which gives the board a faster spring or lift. This is helpful for children who do not have enough weight to fully depress the board. When the fulcrum wheel is moved backward, the tip of the board is lowered to allow for a deeper depression of the board and a longer take-off time. Stronger divers or those with more body weight usually like the fulcrum moved all the way back. The general rule is to be able to get the lift of the board without the feet "blobbling" on the board or the knees straightening too soon or too late for the lift. The many fulcrum settings in-between allow divers of various weights and muscular quickness to adjust the timing of the board lift to their liking. Some divers may prefer different fulcrum adjustments for different dives. Fulcrum adjustment should be corrected while learning the dry approach forward and backward.

Equipment

Board and fulcrum installations may be obtained from many of the fine commercial swimming pool equipment suppliers.

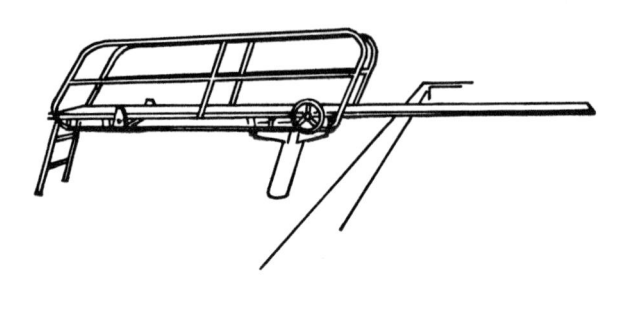

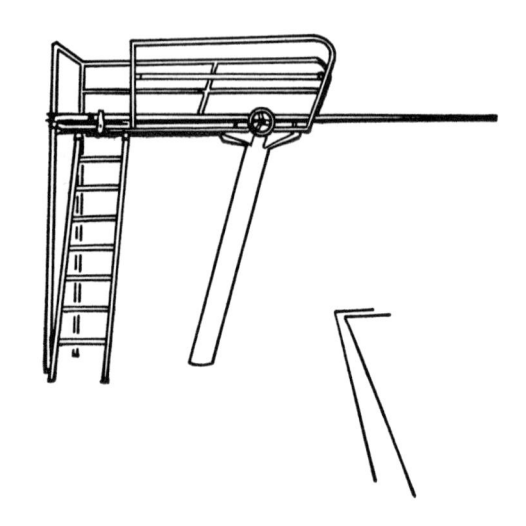

Figure 1. One-Meter and Three-Meter Boards.

THE FUNDAMENTALS OF DIVING

Diving is considered by many teachers and coaches as a highly specialized activity which requires special talent. At the top level of championship diving this may be true; nevertheless, considerable skill and success in diving can be obtained by many people in a relatively short time. As in any sport there are certain prerequisites.

THE ABILITY TO SWIM

It would be foolish to attempt to dive without knowing how to swim. But an additional level of skill in the water is necessary. This is the ability to go downward through the water comfortably. Many beginning divers strain muscles trying in fear to get back to the surface of the water *before* the entire body has actually gone downward through the water. Several jumps into deep water from the side of the pool, holding the body erect until reaching the bottom, should dispel any doubts about the diver's ability to come back to the surface. When the diver comes in contact with the bottom, he should bend his knees and push off the bottom with his feet to surface quickly. The eyes should remain open while going to the bottom. This will also let the diver know how long the process of going down and coming back to the surface will take.

EXHALING IN THE WATER

As diving skill increases, the diver will project himself to the bottom of the pool. It is essential that the diver be able to exhale air, preferably from the nose, while going to the bottom. Holding the breath to the bottom of a pool that is twelve or fourteen feet deep may result in a slight ear drum puncture. Exhaling air while going to the bottom tends to equalize the pressure on the ear and reduces this possibility.

Again, several jumps from the side of the pool into deep water to the bottom while exhaling air will help the beginning diver accomplish this fundamental skill.

A FRONT DIVE FROM THE SIDE OF THE POOL

Diving from a springboard involves a body lift into the air. If the diver cannot perform a plain front dive or racing dive from the side of the pool, progressing to springboard diving is pointless. If this situation exists, begin with a prone, face-down glide into the water by pushing off the side of the pool with the feet, and extending the arms in front of the head.

Next, sit on the side of the pool with the arms overhead and the chin down. Fall into the water and push off with the feet from the side to a gliding position in the water. When this feels comfortable, progress to a front dive from a kneeling position from the side of the pool by lifting the hips and falling forward into the water. The arms are held straight and extended overhead and as the head and arms go through the water, the hips are extended, the forward foot pushes against the pool deck and the knees are straightened for the glide through the water. When this has been achieved, stand at the edge of the pool where the water is deep and bend at the hips. Extend the arms overhead and fall forward into the water pushing gently with the feet. Do not kick the feet backward. As the body falls forward and the extended arms go through the water, extend the hips to achieve a straight body position for the glide. All other dives from the side of the pool, such as the back dive or somersault dive, should be avoided because of the danger of hitting the side wall under water.

BODY POSITIONS IN DIVING

Straight or Lay-Out Position

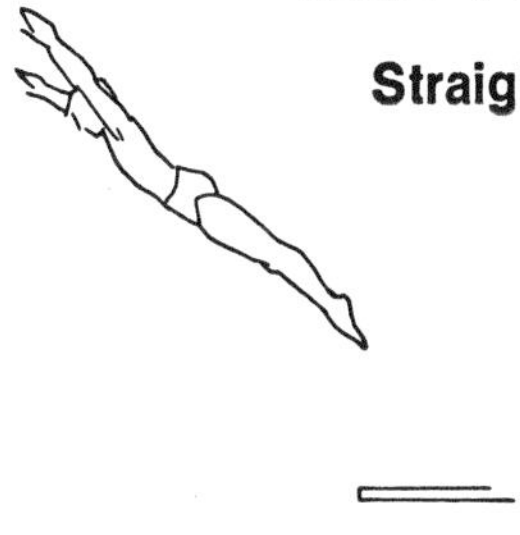

This is the extended position of the body. The legs are straight and in line with the body. The spine is straight, not curved or overarched. The arms are straight and extended overhead close to the sides of the head. The chin is held in line with the spine.

Figure 2. The Straight Position.

Pike Position

In the pike position, the body is bent at the hips and the legs are straight with the toes pointed. The arms are extended forward and the hands usually grasp the backs of the ankles or the calves. The arms may be held straight out to the side. This is called an open pike.

Figure 3. The Pike Position.   Figure 4. The Open Pike Position.

Tuck Position

In the tuck position, the hips and knees are bent and the knees are pulled close to the shoulders by the hands. The knees should be together and the hands grasp the shins between the knees and ankles. The elbows are held close to the legs.

Figure 5. The Tuck Position.

Free Position

This is not a genuine position that is held during the dive, but rather a combination of any of the preceding three positions mentioned. For example, the free position may utilize tuck, pike, or straight positions during somersault twisting movements.

Figure 6. Twisting Dive in the Free Position.

FUNDAMENTAL EXERCISES FOR DIVING

A great degree of flexibility and strength is not needed to perform many of the exciting dives that are seen at every swimming pool and diving competition. Lift into the air from the springboard is achieved by a combination of the press of the feet against the board, ankle extension, straightening of the knees and hips, upward swing of the arms, and the additional lift of the depressed board. To bring all of these factors together demands more practice in timing and control than actual bodily strength. Flexibility of the ankles, shoulders, and hips is more important in diving than flexibility of the back. For these reasons, the physical strength required for diving is less than that for many other sports.

The fundamental exercises presented below are valuable specifically for diving and may be performed without undue punishment. Most of the exercises may be executed on the pool side as part of the warm-up for diving.

Exercises for the Diving Positions

Straight Position

Figure 7. Exercise 1, Straight Position.

Exercise 1 Lie on the stomach with legs straight, ankles extended, and arms extended forward and close to the head. Place the forehead on the floor. Stretch and tense the body. Hold for three seconds.

Figure 8. Exercise 2, Straight Position.

Exercise 2 Stand with the back as straight as possible. Lift the straight arms forward and upward and close to the sides of the head. Rise on to the balls of both feet and stretch the body upward. The knees are kept straight. Hold for three seconds.

Pike Position

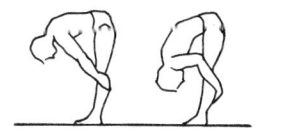

Figure 9. Exercise 3, Pike Position.

Exercise 3 Stand on the floor with the knees straight. Grasp the backs of the legs with the hands while bending the body forward at the hips, keeping the knees straight. Pull against the backs of the legs with the hands. Repeat three times.

Tuck Position

Figure 10. Exercise 4, Tuck Position.

Exercise 4 Sit or lie on the floor. Pull the bent knees up to the chin and grasp the shins with the hands. The toes should be pointed and the knees kept close together. The elbows should be held close to the legs. Hold for three seconds.

Exercise 5 Stand on the floor. Lift one leg with the knee bent. Grasp the shin of the lifted knee with both hands and pull the knee towards the chin as the body leans forward. Hold for three seconds and repeat with opposite leg.

Figure 11. Exercise 5, Tuck Position.

Exercises for Strength

Leg Strength

Exercise 6 Jump rope for a few minutes each day.

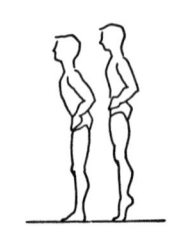

Figure 12. Exercise 6, Jump Rope.

Ankle Strength

Exercise 7 Stand with the feet flat on the floor. Lift both heels as high as possible and return to the floor. The ankles should not bow outward when the heels are lifted. Repeat several times.

Figure 13. Exercise 7, Ankle Strength.

Shoulder and Upper Back Strength

Exercise 8 Kick a handstand with the feet resting against the wall. Stretch and tense the body. Be certain not to place the hands on a wet floor for the handstand.

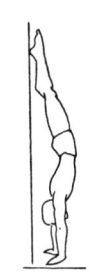

Figure 14. Exercise 8, Shoulder Strength.

Lower Back Strength

Exercise 9 Lie on the stomach, with the arms bent and the chin resting on the hands. Lift both legs, keeping the knees straight, until the knees are off the floor.

Figure 15. Exercise 9, Lower Back Strength.

Abdominal Strength

Exercise 10 Sit on the floor. Place the hands on the floor by the hips. Lift both legs, keeping the knees straight and the toes pointed. Hold the legs in this position for three counts.

Figure 16. Exercise 10, Abdominal Strength.

Exercises for Flexibility

Ankle Flexibility

Exercise 11 Sit on the floor with the legs extended forward and the knees straight and together. Point the toes and pull them back again. Repeat several times.

Figure 17. Exercise 11, Ankle Flexibility.

Hip Flexibility

Exercise 12 Stand in a straddle position with the knees straight and the feet apart. Bend the body at the hips and place the hands on the floor in front of the body. Press the chest as close to the straight legs as possible with a bobbing motion.

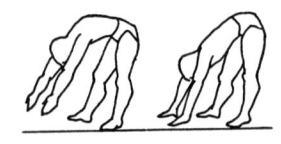

Figure 18. Exercise 12, Hip Flexibility.

Shoulder Flexibility

Exercise 13 Stand in a pike position, with the straight arms extended overhead and the hands resting on a chair or the back end of the diving board. Bounce the chest up and down, keeping the arms straight.

Figure 19. Exercise 13, Shoulder Flexibility.

The exercises presented are not the only exercises that will achieve the goals in preparation for diving, but they represent a good start. Performing most of the exercises a few minutes before each diving session will serve two purposes: (1) the diver will become familiar with the kinesthetic feeling of the body positions used in diving, and (2) the exercises will serve as a warm-up by increasing the body flexibility and strength.

THE APPROACH FORWARD

Now begin with the diving preliminaries. The approach in diving consists of getting to the end of the board while building up forward momentum in preparation for the lift or take-off from the board.

The Steps

The approach consists of three, four or five walking steps towards the end of the board, a hurdle with one leg lifted, a two-foot landing on the end of the board, and a two-foot take-off from the board. During the entire approach until the body has lifted off the board, the eyes are focused downward on the board where the feet are to be placed. All steps in the approach are flat: that is to say, heel-toe steps. Do not remain on the ball of the foot. There is no body lean during the steps, and the knees straighten for a split second during each step as in normal walking. Many beginning divers mistakenly try to gain momentum by galloping or leaning forward as they step toward the end of the board. The arms are usually kept straight and at the sides of the body. Any excessive swinging of the arms may cause a shoulder lean forward and backward which will alter body balance and the angle of take-off.

Generally beginners employ three steps to get to the end of the board; a left step, right step, left step, with the next right leg movement becoming the lift of the right knee or hurdle in preparation for landing and take-off. As diving experience is gained the diver may take four or five steps before the hurdle.

The Hurdle

After the third step, the next right leg movement is the hurdle, or a single right leg lift that brings both feet off the board. The upper right leg is lifted for the hurdle at right angles to the body, with the knee bent, ankle extended, and toe pointed towards the board. The left leg remains straight. The steps and hurdle may be reversed for divers who are left-handed. Any deviation of the correct right angle of the hurdle leg can cause a body lean on take-off. The lift of the right leg, or hurdle, brings both feet off the board to project the body upward. As soon as the feet have left the board, the hurdle leg straightens so that both feet come together with the knees straight. The general rule for the approach is that when the body is lifted off the board the knees are straight and they bend only when contacting the board. During the hurdle, the arms swing forward and upward, close to the body, and in front of the sides of the head. The arms remain upward until the downward fall of the body is felt. The arms then swing sideward and downward so that when both feet land on the end of the board in preparation for take-off, the arms are straight, down and close to the hips and swinging forward and upward. Particular attention should be given to the arms so that on the downward fall of the body in preparation for take-off, they do not swing too far in back of the body to cause a back arch or backward lean. The distance covered on the board for the hurdle should not exceed two feet or be less than ten inches. The eyes remain focused downward on the end of the board for the hurdle.

Figure 20. The Forward Approach Showing the Steps, Hurdle and Body Position in Preparation for Landing on the End of the Board Before Take-Off.

The Take-Off

The take-off is performed with both feet on the board. Previously, during the hurdle, the toes are pointed so that the toes and balls of the feet touch the board first, but the heels should then come down for the flat-footed position. Staying on the balls of the feet will kill the lift of the board and project the legs vigorously over the head during the dive. The maximum lift can be achieved when both feet are flat on the board with the knees bent,

Figure 21. The Forward Approach. Landing on the End of the Board in Preparation for Take-Off, and Take-Off.

the arms are down near the hips and swinging forward and the board is depressed. The shoulders should be in line with the knees, and the body lean should be no more than five degrees forward.

At this point, the eye focus is downward on the water approximately three feet out from the end of the board. The feet should land on the end of the board. The toes should not be hanging over the end of the board on take-off.

The lift from the board, a position in which the feet are flat on the board, the arms are down, and the leaning body is in direct alignment, is probably the single most important factor in the success and safety of the ensuing dive. It is impossible to practice these elements of the approach too often. If the proper position is achieved, the board will project the diver at least three feet forward so that the dive will be not only more successful, but also safe. Any greater lean forward will project the body forward in the water, and of course any body lean backward will bring the diver closer to the board.

Contrary to the belief of inexperienced divers, leaning in closer to the board does not make the dive worth more points. The generally accepted distance between the end of the board and the point of entrance into the water from the end of the board by water is approximately two to three feet.

On the take off from the board, the straight arms swing forward and upward, close to the sides of the head, and the knees and the hips straighten so that the body is extended. The heels rise from the board first, and then the toes, after pressing against the board. Without exception, this occurs in every good dive, no matter which way the body moves after leaving the board.

All of the elements in the approach should be practiced many times on land, and then on the board with a feet-first jump into the water, until a feeling of consistency in performance and familiarity with the board is achieved. The dry approach is also very valuable as a preliminary practice to diving. It increases control and surefootedness on the board.

The Forward Dry Approach or Practice Approach Forward

After the forward approach has been achieved on land and on the board with a feet-first entry into the water, the diver is ready to proceed to the forward dry approach. By now, the steps and hurdle should be covering about the same distance on each attempt. The diver should then walk to the forward end of the board and turn around. From here, take three steps, a hurdle, and lift going towards the back of the board. He should then turn around again, back up approximately six inches and mark the spot on the board where he is standing. This is his starting point. The additional six inches is for a margin of error in the travelling distance of the steps and hurdle.

From here, proceed to a dry approach forward which consists of three steps, a low hurdle, landing, and take-off, *without* the body lean forward, so as to land back on the board. Kill the lift of the board by bending the knees quickly as the board rises for the lift. Proceed carefully with the forward dry approach. Do not take a series of bounces on the board, as this will throw the body out of control.

Figure 22. The Dry Approach Forward, Showing Steps, Hurdle, Landing in Preparation for Take-Off, Take-Off, Returning to the Board, and Killing the Lift of the Board.

Common Faults in the Forward Approach and Take-Off

Figure 23. Steps Too Long in the Forward Approach.

Steps Too Long

Taking steps longer than normal walking steps may cause a body lean backward toward the board during the hurdle and take-off from the board. It will also change the spacing of the steps and hurdle.

Figure 24. Hopping Before the Hurdle in the Forward Approach.

Hopping Before The Hurdle

Hopping on the step before the hurdle leg lifts upward will cause the diver to lose control of the upright position on the hurdle. This in turn will force the body to lean outward on the take-off. Any hopping while the diver is stepping toward the end of the board may also result in slipping on the board. All steps should be heel-toe steps.

Figure 25. Hooked Hurdle in the Forward Approach.

Hooked Hurdle

When performing the hurdle, the diver should be able to see his right knee and right toe below the knee in front of him. If the right foot hooks the back of the left leg on the hurdle, it may cause the diver to bend at the hips which will alter the timing of the lift from the board as well as the angle of take-off.

Figure 26. Kicked Hurdle in the Forward Approach.

Kicked Hurdle

If the diver can see not only his right knee and right toe on the hurdle, but the entire lower leg, he is kicking the hurdle leg too far forward. This will cause an inconsistent traveling distance on the hurdle.

Figure 27. Hurdle Leg Held Up Too Long in the Forward Approach.

Hurdle Leg Held Up Too Long

Once the hurdle has accomplished its job, that is, to lift the feet and body off the board, the hurdle leg should be straightened immediately so that both legs are straight and the feet are together in the air, ready to land on the board in preparation for take-off. Holding the hurdle leg up too long will result in an unbalanced landing on the end of the board and a body twist during the take-off and dive.

Figure 28. Pounding the Board in the Forward Approach.

Pounding the Board

Pounding the board occurs when the knees are still bent after the hurdle when the feet land on the board in preparation for take-off. This has the same effect as killing the lift of the board on take-off. The knees should be straight while the diver is in the air after the hurdle, and bend only when the feet contact the board.

Figure 29. Arms Too Far Backward on Landing Before Take-Off on the Forward Approach.

Arms Too Far Backward on Landing Before Take-Off

After the hurdle in preparation for take-off, the arms should swing sideward and downward. Dropping the arms backward on the downward swing will cause a body lean backward. The body should be in the erect position for the entire forward approach.

Figure 30. Sitting on the Take-Off in the Forward Approach.

Sitting on the Take-Off

On the take-off from the board, the knees should bend enough to allow the diver to join the timing of the board for maximum lift. Too great a bend of the knees will alter this timing and cause the diver to lose the lift of the board. Bending the knees too deeply may also cause a forward shoulder lean on take-off.

Figure 31. Remaining on the Toes for the Take-Off in the Forward Approach.

Remaining on the Toes for Take-Off

The take-off should come from a flat-footed stance on the board. The heels rise first, then the toes. Staying on the balls of the feet for the landing and take-off eliminates the straightening of the knees and the hips for the take-off and projects the body forward on the dive. It also throws the legs vigorously over the head during the dive.

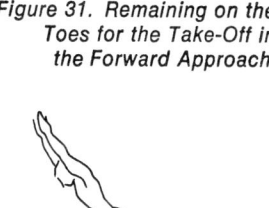

Figure 32. Forward Lean on Take-Off in the Forward Approach.

Forward Lean on Take-Off

This is caused when the diver leans his shoulders too far forward on the take-off. Many beginning divers lean out over the board in their anxiety to tilt the body towards the water for the entry.

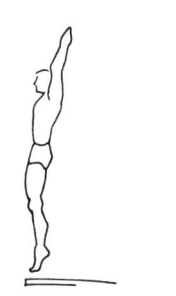

Figure 33. Backward Lean on the Take-Off in the Forward Approach.

Backward Lean on Take-Off

This is caused when the diver rocks his shoulders backward on the steps or hurdle and presses his hips forward on the take-off from the board. On the forward approach, the backward lean on take-off is dangerous and should be avoided by keeping the shoulders over the knees.

Figure 34. Failure to Straighten the Knees Completely on Take-Off in the Forward Approach.

Failure to Straighten the Knees Completely on Take-Off

On the take-off, the knees should be completely straightened before the feet leave the board or before any part of the dive is initiated. Failure to straighten the knees completely on take-off will cause the feet to slip or skid off the board and the body will drift back in towards the board during the dive.

THE APPROACH BACKWARD

The body is held erect with a slight lean forward from the feet to the shoulders. The knees are held straight to offset the downward dip of the end of the board. This slight lean forward will prevent the diver from losing his balance and falling backward off the board. The arms are usually held forward in front of the shoulders to maintain the balance until the feet have been properly placed on the end of the board. Once again, the eye focus is downward on the back end of the board, *but the head is held in line with the body.* The feet should be flat, with no more than three-fifths of the length of the foot extended off the end of the board. This means that the ball of the foot and approximately one-half to one inch of the transverse arch is on the board supporting the body weight.

Standing Position Facing Backward

Figure 35. Placing the Feet on the End of the Board in the Backward Approach.

Many teachers and coaches of diving do not introduce the backward approach until after the back dive itself has been achieved. However, the basic standing and lifting fundamentals can be practiced before the back dive has been attempted. All fundamental positions and arm swings should be performed on land first before going to the board.

After maintaining balance in the standing position on the end of the board, the diver lowers his straight arms to his sides while keeping an erect body position with a slight lean forward. The knees are completely straight.

Arm Swing and Ankle Extension

On the backward approach off the board, only the arms initiate the movement, and the ankles extend until the knees bend and straighten to lift the body backward off the board. At first beginning divers do not teeter or rock the board or take more than one lift of the heels in this position.

From the back standing position on the end of the board with the arms down at the sides, the arms swing sideward and upward as the heels are lifted with the knees held straight. The arms then swing sideward and downward as the heels are lowered. The arms continue to swing forward and upward. The knees are bent with the body held upright, and as the arms swing upward, the knees straighten and the feet press downward against the board for the lift off the board. On the lift-off, the arms should remain close to the sides of the head.

The backward approach should be practiced first on land, to gain coordination of the arm swing and heel lift and knee bend.

Figure 36. The Approach Backward, showing Arm Movement, Heel Lift, Knee Bend, and Body Position.

The Back Dry Approach or Practice Approach Backward

The back dry approach is used to time the lift of the board for back take-off dives. All fundamentals should be practiced on dry land first before attempting the back dry approach on the board.

From the balanced standing position backward, the straight arms lift sideward and upward and the diver lifts his heels to the extended ankle position. If the ankles bow outward, the heels have been lifted too high for balanced extension. The arms then swing downward as the heels lower and the knees and hips bend. The body remains upright. The arms continue to swing forward and upward to a position close to the sides of the head and the heels lift again to an extended ankle position. The knees and hips straighten, the toes press downward against the board, and the body is lifted into the air. As in the forward approach, the body becomes a tensed projectile without a body arch. When attempting the back dry approach, first on dry land, and then on the board, be certain to jump forward so as not to land too close to the end of the board. After the body is lifted into the air and the diver lands on the board (with the balls of the feet touching first, and then the heels), he should kill the lift of the board by bending the knees quickly and keeping the feet flat on the board.

Figure 37. The Back Dry Approach or Practice Approach Backward.

Common Faults in the Backward Approach

Figure 38. Feet Extended Too Far Off the End of the Board in the Backward Approach.

Feet Extended Too Far Off the End of the Board

If the feet are extended too far off the end of the board, balance cannot be maintained. The body may bend at the hips and a body lean forward or backward may occur during the take-off and dive.

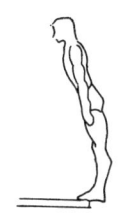

Figure 39. Hips Bent in the Backward Approach.

Hips Bent

The hips should be held in line with the body. If the hips are bent on the back standing position, the angle of take-off and the dive will not be consistent.

Figure 40. Arm Swing Backward in the Back Approach.

Arm Swing Backward

After the sideward lift of the arms, they swing down to the sides of the body. The arms then continue to swing forward and upward for the take-off from the board. If the arms swing too far in back of the body, the hips will bend and the shoulders will lean forward over the board.

Figure 41. Crow Hop in the Back Approach.

Crow Hop

This expression refers to a double take-off or bounce on the board from the back approach position. The preliminary lift of the heels and arm swing sideward should not lift the feet of the diver off the board. If this occurs, the timing of the board is lost and the diver's feet may shift position on the end of the board.

Figure 42. Knees Bent on Take-Off in the Backward Approach.

Knees Bent on Take-Off

The same fundamentals apply to the lift or take-off from the back approach position as from the forward approach. The knees must straighten first before any part of the dive is executed or the feet are lifted off the board. Beginning a tuck position or bending the body for a pike position before the knees have been straightened on take-off will cause the diver to drift in toward the board during the dive.

THE ENTRY

The entry is a term used to describe the finish of the dive when the body passes through the water. There are only two types of entries into the water in diving; the head-first entry and the feet-first entry. In both entry positions the body is completely extended, with the head held in line with the spine and the chin tucked in.

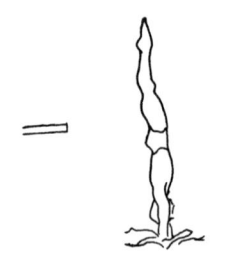

Figure 43. Head-First Entry into the Water.

In the head-first entry into the water, the arms are extended overhead in line with the head, so the hands and arms can make an entry path through the water for the head and body. The body is not arched, the legs are straight, and the toes should be pointed.

In the feet-first entry, the straight arms are held along the sides of the body. The pointed toes and feet are employed to make an entry path through the water for the body. The body is held tensed and erect, with the head in line with the back.

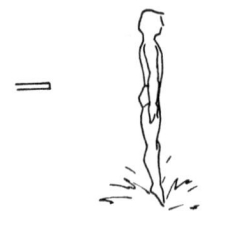

Figure 44. Feet-First Entry into the Water.

A good entry passes through the water approximately two to four feet from the tip of the board. The angle of entry when the body begins to pass through the water should be no more than five degrees under or over the vertical line. Any deviation from this angle will result not only in a poorly executed dive but also in the probability that some part of the body or legs will slap the water.

A clean, crisp, controlled body entry into the water should be one of the objectives of every dive from the beginning of the diver's learning experience. In the event that a dive goes out of control, the problem of saving the dive above and under the water is discussed in Chapter 4.

Entry positions may be practiced on the land (see Exercises 1 and 2) and also from the side of the pool by pushing off with the feet and gliding through the water. Many beginning divers tend to relax the body when it passes through the water. This feeling of relaxation should be replaced with a feeling of body extension and mental awareness. The total effort of a dive does not finish until the diver has reached the bottom of the pool and begins to surface. In the head-first entry, the hands are held in front of the head, going through the water in preparation for touching the bottom.

Most experienced divers consider their entry to be good when there is a lack of water splash as the body passes through the surface of the water. This is described as a "soft" or "clean" entry.

Common Faults in the Entry into the Water

Short Entry

This is a term used for an entry which is less than five degrees under the vertical line. A short entry stings the front of the body on the forward entry and the back of the body on the backward entry.

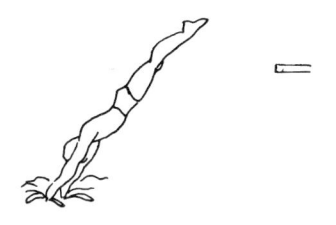

Figure 45a. Short Entry in the Forward Dive.

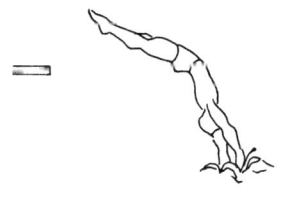

45b. Short Entry in the Backward Dive.

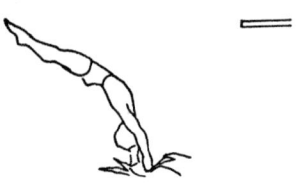

Figure 46a. Long Entry in the Forward Dive.

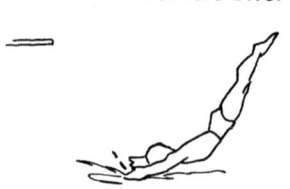

46b. Long Entry in the Backward Dive.

Long Entry

The long entry is one in which the legs or body are over five degrees of the vertical line. A long entry on the forward dives may result in a back arch and may strain the muscles of the back. A long entry on back dives will sting the front of the body and legs.

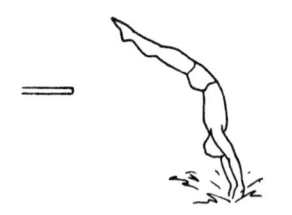

Figure 47. Back Arch Entry.

Back Arch Entry

In all entries, head first or feet first, the back should be flat. If the back is arched, it may cause back strain and will result in excessive splash during entry.

Figure 48. Head Up on Entry.

Head Up on Entry

The chin may be extended during certain dives but as the hands hit the water at the beginning of the entry, the chin should be tucked in, to bring the head in line with the spine. If the head is held up for entry into the water, the face will slap the water.

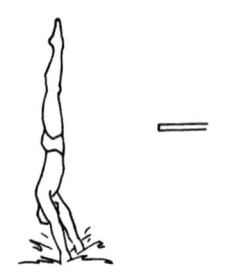

Figure 49. Arms Low on Entry.

Arms Low on Entry

On head-first entries, the arms should be straight, overhead, and in line with the body. Dropping the arms forward for the entry allows the head to receive the initial force or "hit" of the water.

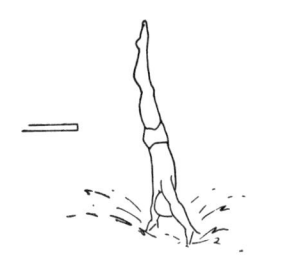

Figure 50. Arms Sideward on Entry.

Arms Sideward on Entry

After performing a dive, many beginning divers fail to bring the arms close to the sides of the head for entry. Even if the chin is in the proper position, keeping the arms sideward for entry will cause the head to receive the initial force or "hit" of the water.

Knees Bent on Entry

Except in instances when a dive must be saved, the knees should be straight for the entry.

Figure 51. Knees Bent on Entry.

THE CATEGORIES OF DIVES

One-meter and three-meter springboard diving is divided into five categories. The category of the dive is used to describe the direction of the body off the board. The four body positions in diving (tuck, pike, straight, and free), previously described, are used in all of the diving categories. The five categories of diving are as follows:
1. Forward
2. Backward
3. Reverse
4. Inward
5. Twisting

THE FORWARD CATEGORY

The forward category includes any dive in which the diver uses a forward approach with the front of the body facing the end of the board, and performs a dive in which the front of the body leans toward the water or rotates toward the water for the entry. Ex-

Figure 52. Forward Dive, Straight Position.

amples of the forward category are the forward dive or any forward somersaulting dive. Forward dives may be executed in any of the three body positions (tuck, pike, or straight). Forward somersault dives may be executed with a head-first or feet-first entry. The number of somersaults determines the type of entry into the water. For example, a forward dive with one somersault would use a feet-first entry, and a forward dive with one and one-half somersaults would use a head-first entry. The additional one-half somersault changes the body from the feet-first to the head-first entry position.

THE BACKWARD CATEGORY

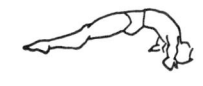

Figure 53. Back Dive, Straight Position.

The backward category includes any dive which is performed from a back approach at the end of the board, and in which the shoulders lean backward or the body rotates backward from the board toward the water for the entry. Examples of the backward category are the backward dive or any backward somersaulting dive. Backward dives may be executed in either the tuck, pike, or straight body position. Backward somersault dives may be performed with either a feet-first or head-first entry. The number of somersaults determines the type of entry into the water. For example, a back dive with one somersault would use a feet-first entry. A back dive with one and one-half somersaults would use a head-first entry into the water.

THE REVERSE CATEGORY

The reverse category includes any dive that begins with a forward approach and take-off from the board when the shoulders lean backward or rotate backward towards the water for the entry. Examples of the reverse

Figure 54. Reverse Dive, Straight Position.

category are the back dive or any backward somersaulting dive from the forward approach and take-off from the board. Reverse dives may be executed in the tuck, pike, or straight body positions. Reverse somersaulting dives may use either a head-first or feet-first entry into the water.

THE INWARD CATEGORY

The inward category includes any dive in which the diver uses a backward approach and take-off from the end of the board and the shoulders lean forward or rotate forward towards the water for the entry. Examples of the inward category are the forward dive from the back take-off or any forward somersaulting dive from the back approach and take-off from the board. Inward dives may be executed in the tuck, pike, or straight position. Inward somersaulting dives may use either a head-first or feet-first entry into the water, depending on the number of somersaults.

Figure 55. Inward Dive, Straight Position.

The somersault dives in the four categories mentioned are defined as feet-first entry dives when the body completes a single, double, or triple somersault and the feet enter the water first upon completion of the dive. The one and one-half, two and one-half, and three and one-half somersault dives are defined as head-first entries into the water. The additional one-half somersault changes the position of the body from the feet-first entry position to the head-first entry position.

THE TWISTING CATEGORY

The twisting category includes any dive in the preceding categories to which an additional side axis twist of the body has been added. Once a twist of the body has been included in the dive, that dive is included in the twisting category. For example, a forward dive in the straight position with the body performing a half-twist in the air to a head-first backward entry into the water would be in the twisting category and defined as a "forward dive, one-half twist, straight position." Twisting dives may be performed in the tuck, pike, straight, or free position. Most somersaulting dives that include a body twist are listed as in the free position.

All dives which may be performed from the springboard are listed and rated according to their degree of difficulty by the Amateur Athletic Union, the National Collegiate Athletic Association, and the Division for Girls' and Womens' Sports of the American Association of Health, Physical Education, and Recreation. Chapter 6 includes a brief explanation of the rating of dives and the judging of diving. A diving sheet showing the current ratings in the degree of difficulty of each dive is included.

Figure 56. Forward Dive, One-Half Twist, Straight Position.

FUNDAMENTAL TO ADVANCED DIVES

Fundamental dives are those which do not include a multiple change of body position in the air.

Fundamental Dives

Beginning dives are those dives in which the body is fixed in one position and held until entry into the water. Only the arm direction and head position change in these dives. For example:

1. **Forward dive, straight position.**

2. **Back dive, straight position.**

Next are those dives which involve one body movement during flight, as well as a change in arm direction and head placement.

3. Forward dive, one-half twist, straight position.

The basic single-position dives in the inward and reverse categories are more difficult for the inexperienced diver, so the next progression after (1) the forward dive, (2) the back dive, and (3) the forward dive, one-half twist, straight position is to those dives which involve two body movements during flight as well as a change in arm direction and head placement: for example, the forward dive in the pike position. Once the forward dive, pike position is under control, the diver may progress to the inward category.

4. Inward dive, pike position.

The reverse dive in either the straight or pike position cannot be achieved until more experience on the board has been gained by the diver. This dive requires a consistent forward approach and lift off from the board to guarantee safety. Nevertheless, it is included in the diver's beginning list.

5. Reverse dive, straight position.

When fundamental dives have been achieved, the diver has a complete list of the required dives: that is, one dive from each category in either the straight or pike position. This selection is required for diving competition. The diver must also have one additional dive from each category and one extra dive from any category of his choice, for a total of six optional dives. His total performance list would include eleven dives: five required dives and six optional dives.

Intermediate Dives, Optional List

Intermediate dives include dives with more than one body movement and somersaulting dives.

6. Forward dive, one somersault, tuck position.

7. Back dive, one somersault, tuck position.

8. Forward dive, one and one-half somersaults, tuck position.

8a. Forward dive, one and one-half somersaults, pike position.

9. Inward dive, one somersault, tuck position.

10. Reverse dive, one somersault, tuck position.

11. Forward dive, one and one-half somersaults, one-half twist, tuck position.

For most youngsters or students, the preceding list will allow the diver to progress to more difficult dives while maintaining his total list of eleven dives. The diver's progression to the more difficult dives depends at this point upon individual differences of strength, timing, control, understanding, desire, experience, the ability to concentrate, and available teaching or coaching.

Advanced Dives

Advanced dives are those which involve more than one body rotation or somersault before entry into the water, or one body rotation or somersault with one or two twists of the body. The preceding six optional dives are considered advanced when performed in the straight position or when an additional one-half somersault is added to bring the dive to a head-first entry into the water. For the actual degree of difficulty, refer to the diving sheet.

WHERE TO BEGIN— ONE METER

Once the diver is familiar with the body positions in diving and can perform them on the floor or pool deck, he is ready to jump off the board and perform first a tuck position to a feet-first entry; then pike position to a feet-first entry; and finally a straight position to a feet-first entry. After the diver has gained a consistent dry approach both forward and backward, he is ready for the mechanics of the beginning dives with the head-first entry into the water.

The forward dive is a good one with which to begin since it can be performed from the side of the pool. At first, the diver's main concern is how to get his body tilted towards the water for the head-first entry from a greater height than that of pool side. Remember that the steps, hurdle, landing and takeoff in the forward approach are engaged to project the diver upward and slightly outward off the board, with the body tensed and in the straight position, and with the arms upward, straight, and close to the sides of the head. This take-off not only allows a lift off the board, but a flight pattern which will "top" when the body has stopped lifting but has not yet begun to fall. At this specific point—the top, or slightly before top—the diver's arm motion, shoulder tilt towards the water, and head placement will tilt his body correctly toward the water for the head-first entry. Beginning divers at first will not believe this will occur and will kick the legs upward or bend the body to try to achieve the head-first entry.

For each dive presented, a dry land practice is suggested and a progression of the mechanics of the dive from the standing position on the end of the board. Beginning with these fundamentals should help the diver to avoid many slapping entries while he is gaining experience on the board.

BEGINNING DIVES, ONE METER: REQUIRED LIST

1. Forward Dive, Straight Position

Dry Land Practice

Stand on the pool deck with the body erect and the arms straight down at the sides of the body. The chin is held in line with the spine. Swing both arms forward and upward and close to the sides of the head. The palms of the hands are facing each other. Lower or sweep the arms sideward with the palms of the hands facing the floor. Lift one straight leg with the toe pointed slightly backward and touch the floor in back of the other foot. Swing the arms directly overhead and return the leg that is lifted backward to the standing position. The chin remains in line with the spine for the entire practice position.

From the Standing Position on the End of the Board

Stand on the end of the board facing forward with the arms down at the sides of the body. Do not teeter on the board or take a bounce. Swing the straight arms forward and upward to the sides of the head with the palms of the hands facing each other. Keep the body straight and tensed with the chin tucked in and begin falling off the board. Immediately sweep the arms sideward with the palms of the hands facing downward and the eye focus is on the point of entry into the water. When the body weight is off the feet and the body is approximately parallel with the board, pull the straight arms quickly overhead with the palms facing forward. Lift (do not kick) the straight legs upward, tuck the chin slightly downward and tense the body for entry into the water. Keep the body tense until the hands have touched the bottom of the pool. This standing forward dive in the straight position will result in a slightly short entry but the feeling of tilt toward the water will be experienced by the diver.

Figure 57. Forward Dive, Straight Position from a Standing Position on the End of the Board.

From the Forward Approach

Next, proceed to the forward approach with a low hurdle and slight lift-off from the board and perform the forward dive in the straight position. Gradually increase the lift of the hurdle leg and attain maximum lift-off from the board, keeping the dive under control. The head *does not* lift upward at the top of the dive when the arms sweep sideward. The chin remains in line with the spine during the entire dive. Remember that the take-off from the board should be executed with the body straight, knees straight, arms straight and upward, and a shoulder lean no more than five degrees upon leaving the board. This will allow the diver to reach the top, lower the arms sideward, and tilt the body towards the water for the entry without traveling too far out away from the board.

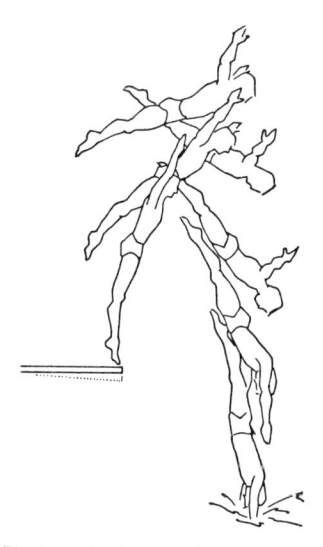

Figure 58. Forward Dive, Straight Position, Showing Lift Off The Board, Top of Flight, Arm Sweep Sideward, Shoulder Lean Toward the Water, Chin Tucked In, and the Tensed Body Position for the Head-First Entry.

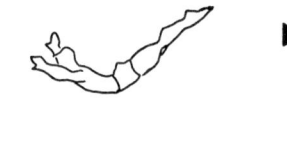

Figure 59. Lifting the Head at the Top in the Forward Dive, Straight Position.

Forward Dive, Straight Position:
▶ **What Can Go Wrong**

Lifting the Head at the Top. Lifting the chin and looking upward at the top of the dive will create an overarched back and possible short entry by delaying the shoulder tilt toward the water.

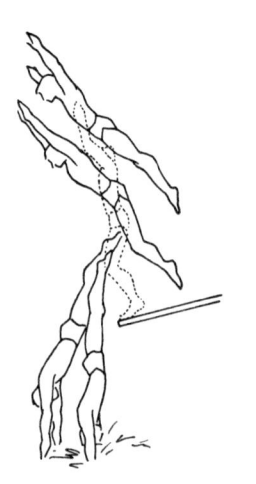

Figure 60. Drift in the Forward Dive, Straight Position.

Drift. Drift back over the board is caused by the diver lifting or kicking the feet upward before the knees have been straightened for the take-off from the board. This is a serious error and can cause the diver to drift backward far enough to hit the board. It should be corrected at the beginning of the diver's learning experience. He should return to more practice on the forward approach with a feet-first jump into the water.

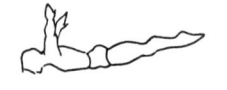

Pulling the Arms Too Far Backward at the Top. This creates a back arch and possible short entry into the water. It causes a less artistic dive.

Figure 61. Pulling the Arms Too Far Backward at the Top of the Forward Dive, Straight Position.

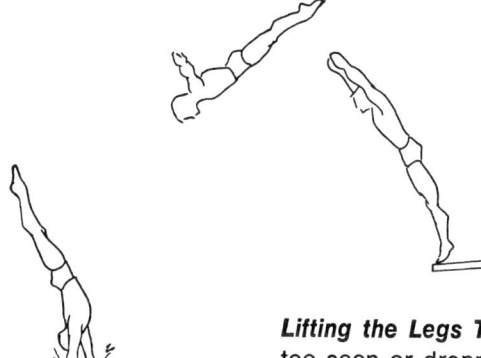

Figure 62. Lifting the Legs Too Soon on the Forward Dive, Straight Position.

Lifting the Legs Too Soon. Lifting the legs too soon or dropping the shoulders toward the water before the top of the dive will cause the diver to overshoot the dive and result in a long entry into the water.

★ Saving the Forward Dive, Straight Position

Short Entry. If the dive is not tilted toward the water in the vertical position in preparation for entry, a short or flat entry will occur. If this is expected, as the diver feels his legs are as low as his shoulders during the downward falling, he should lower his head as far as possible and pull the bent knees up to the chest. The arms are kept out in front of the face to absorb the shock of the water on the face.

Long Entry. If the heels are lifted or kicked upward too soon after leaving the board on the forward dive, the legs will swing too far over the head during the dive and entry into the water. The diver should immediately bring the arms together over the head, keeping the chin up, and look for the water. At the point of contact with the water, he should quickly tuck the chin in as far as possible. As the body passes through the water, bend at the hips so that a forward roll is performed on the entry into the water. The forward roll is *below* the surface of the water, and not before the entry. This will prevent back strain and the stinging of the back of the legs on contact with the water.

2. Back Dive, Straight Position

Dry Land Practice

Stand on the pool side, with the body erect and the arms straight down at the sides. Swing the arms sideward and lift the heels, keeping the knees straight. Swing the arms downward, lower the heels to the floor, and slightly bend the knees. Swing the arms forward and upward, close to the sides of the head, with the palms facing each other; straighten the knees; and lift the heels so that the weight of the body is on the balls of the feet, to simulate take-off from the board. Next, lower the arms sideward with the palms of the hands facing upward, and stretch the chin backward with an outward lift of the chest. Then pull the arms directly overhead and pull the chin in, in line with the spine. Hold the back straight and tense.

From the Standing Position on the End of the Board

From the back approach position, standing on the end of the board with the arms straight down at the sides, lift the arms overhead and close to the sides of the head without teetering the board or taking a bounce. Stretch the body upward, lifting the chest outward, and bend backward until the body falls backward off the board to a head-first entry into the water. Do not bend the knees during the fall off backward. Look for the water while falling and, without rounding the upper back on entry, tuck the chin in so that the face will not experience a slap on the water upon entry. Do not teeter or bounce the board on take-off until you are able to keep the body tense while falling backward off the board. When leaving the board, the toes should be pointed and the feet should be pressed downward so that the legs will not swing over the head. When this has been achieved with control, proceed through the arm motions of the back approach and take-off without the lift of the board.

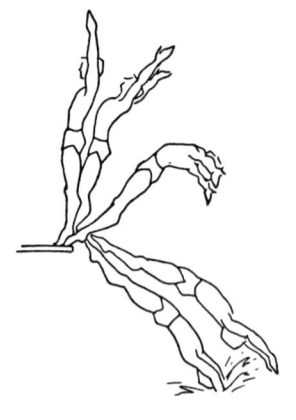

Figure 63. Falling Backward Off the Board in the Back Dive, Straight Position.

Back Dive, Straight Position from the Back Approach

When the diver fully understands the feeling of the straight back, arm movement and chin placement, and can fall off the board backward to the back entry into the water with good control, he may proceed to a back dive with a lift-off from the board.

The backward approach and take-off is the same as described in Chapter 2, with a five degree lean backward. At the top of the lift or slightly before the top, the arms sweep or lower sideward, with the palms of the hands facing upward, and the chin is stretched backward to allow the diver to see the water at the point of entry. The body is held straight and tensed, with the knees straight and the toes pointed. When the arms lower sideward at the top and the chin stretches backward so the diver can see the water, there is a slight chest lift, but not a full body arch. When the diver sees the water and can feel the downward motion, he immediately pulls both arms from the sideward position to overhead and close to the head and tucks in the chin in line with the spine for entry into the water. As the diver gains experience in judging the distance to the water and his falling speed, he will be able to pull his arms overhead in preparation for an entry at about board level. When tucking in the chin for entry, the diver should be certain not to round his shoulders, which will flatten the entry and cause the shoulders to slap the water.

It is important that the knees straighten with the hips in line with the legs on take-off before the feet are lifted off the board. Lifting the feet off the board before the knees straighten, or arching the back before the take-off will cause the body to drift in toward the board. The entire sequence of the take-off should be completed before any part of the dive is begun.

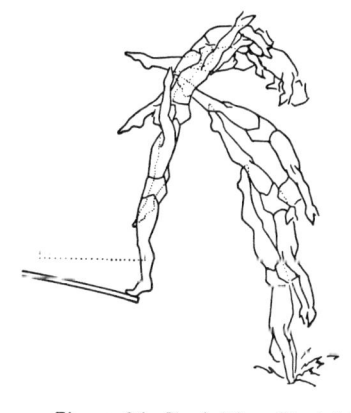

Figure 64. Back Dive, Straight Position, Showing the Lift-Off, Arm Sweep at the Top, and Arm and Head Position on Entry into the Water.

On subsequent back dives, the diver may gain additional lift from the board by slightly teetering on the board during the back approach sequence. This is done by lifting and lowering the heels while standing at attention facing backward on the end of the board, to get the board moving up and down slightly. On approximately the second or third teeter, the arms lift sideward in preparation for take-off. The toes should not leave the board during any part of the teetering movement. Dry land practice is suggested before incorporating the teeter with the back dive.

▶ Back Dive, Straight Position: What Can Go Wrong

Figure 65. Stretching the Head Backward Before Take-Off on the Back Dive, Straight Position.

Stretching the Head Backward Before Take-Off. This will cause greater body rotation backward than is needed for a back dive. The body will rotate or somersault to a front slap entry. It may also cause drift back in toward the board during the dive. Keep the chin in line with the back until the feet have left the board.

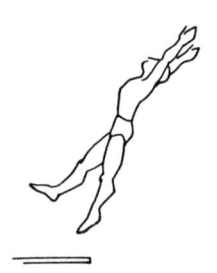

Figure 66. Kicking the Feet Off the Board in the Back Dive, Straight Position.

Kicking the Feet Off the Board. On the take-off the feet should press downward against the board. Kicking the feet off the board before total lift-off will usually bend the body at the hips and cause too much rotation backward, as well as drift back in toward the board.

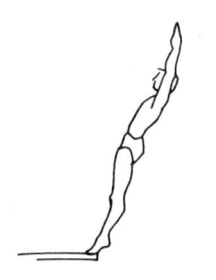

Figure 67. Too Much Shoulder Lean Backward on Take-Off in the Back Dive, Straight Position.

Too Much Shoulder Lean Backward on Take-Off. This will cause the diver to enter the water too far out away from the board. It may also cause a shallow or short entry because the shoulders are not able to tilt toward the water for the vertical entry.

Overarch of the Body at the Top of the Dive. At the top of the lift, when the arms swing or lower sideward, the body and legs should be held tight and as straight as possible. Beginning divers tend to bend their knees and drop their feet toward the water when they stretch their head backward at the top of the lift. This may result in a short entry and a slap to the back of the legs on entry into the water.

Figure 68. Overarch of the Back at the Top of the Back Dive, Straight Position.

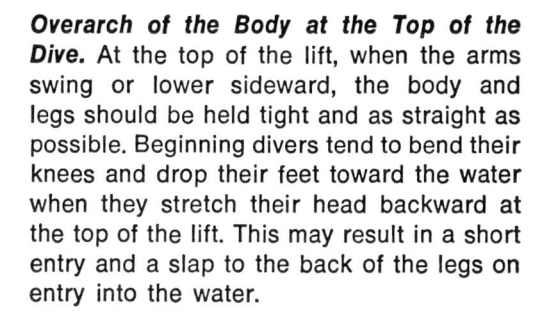

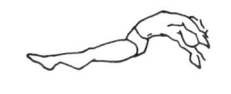

Body Pike. Bending the body during any part of the back dive in the straight position will have the same effect as spinning the body into a backward rotation, which causes a long entry and a slap on the water to the front of the body. It may also cause a complete somersault backward to the feet-first entry.

Figure 69. Body Pike on the Back Dive, Straight Position.

★ **Saving the Back Dive, Straight Position**

Short Entry. A short entry on the back dive will slap the back and the back of the legs. Do not fold or relax the body. If the diver can see the water before he hits it, he should at the point of entry tuck the chin down as far as possible and bend slightly at the hips as the body passes through the water. The hip bend is performed under the surface of the water, not before the entry. If he cannot see the water on a short entry backward, it is best to stretch the body as straight as possible to eliminate a back arch, tuck in the chin, keep the arms close to the sides of the head.

Long Entry. The long entry on the back dive occurs when the head is thrown back too soon on take-off from the board when the body bends at the hips during the dive, or when the shoulders lean backward too far off the board on take-off. Usually the diver can see the water on the long entry, but the body is rotating backward quickly and the dive becomes a three-quarter somersault to a slap entry on the front of the body. Pulling the chin inward as far as possible will save the face from a slap against the water. If the diver is high enough above the water when he feels the rotating movement, and can see the water, he should bend the knees and pull them in close to the chest to complete that rotation backward and enter the water in the feet-first position. If the diver is not high enough above the water to save the dive with a feet-first entry, it is best to tuck in the chin and keep the extended position of the body to "spoon" into the water forward.

3. Forward Dive, One-Half Twist, Straight Position

The forward dive with one-half twist in the straight position is a one-half side axis rotation of the body from the forward dive to the back entry into the water in the vertical position. For the beginning diver it is difficult to master, but does not necessarily demand diving experience. It is relatively safe to attempt without maximum lift from the board or a perfectly performed forward approach and take-off.

The arms swing forward and upward as in the forward dive. The head is held in line with the spine with the chin tucked. The eyes are focused downward. On the sideward lowering of the arms from the overhead position, the shoulders turn at right angles to the board. The diver executes a one-quarter turn of the body. During the first quarter turn of the body, the chin remains tucked in and facing the water with the eye focus downward on the water at the point of entry. The shoulders and body complete an additional one-quarter turn and the head rolls backward with the chin stretched backward to look for the water as in the top of the back dive. The arms remain sideward. The arms then lift directly overhead and the chin is tucked in for the back entry into the water. The body remains straight and tensed for the entire dive. The feet are held lower than the chest during the dive.

Dry Land Practice

Stand on the left leg with the left leg straight. Stretch the right leg backward with the right toe pointed and touching the pool deck about one foot in back of the left leg. The legs may be reversed for a one-half twist practice to the left. The entire weight of the body is over the left leg. Swing both arms forward and upward, close to the sides of the head, and keep the eye focus downward on the pool deck. Swing both arms to the side position, and execute a one-quarter turn to the right by pivoting on the left foot. In the sideward position, the right arm should be held higher than the left arm for the twist. Continue turning the shoulders and body until a one-half turn or twist has been completed. The arms are stretched out to the sides with both arms parallel. The weight of the body remains on the left foot. When the half turn has been completed, the right toe is pointed on the pool deck in front of the body, and the chin is stretched backward as in the back dive position.

From a Standing Position on the End of the Board

Next, the diver should proceed to the board and stand on the end of the board in the forward position. Place the straight right leg backward on the diving board with the pointed toe touching the board and execute the dry land practice for the one-half twist, and fall backward into the water in the back entry position.

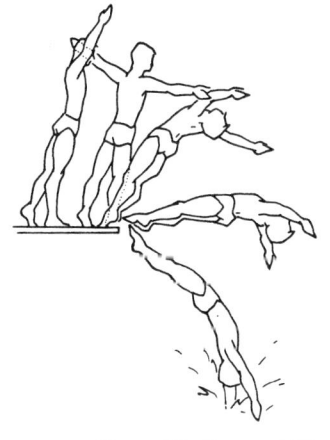

Figure 70. Forward Dive, One-Half Twist, Straight Position, From a Standing Position on the End of the Board.

When the body turn, arm swing, and head placement are fully understood and coordinated from the standing position, the diver may perform a forward dive, one-half twist in the straight position with the forward approach and take-off.

Forward Dive, One-Half Twist, Straight Position from the Forward Approach

On the forward dive, one-half twist, the first quarter turn is executed before the top of the lift, and held to the top of the dive. At that point, the body executes the second quarter turn or twist to complete the twist and place the body in the back dive entry position with the body straight. The legs should be held lower than the shoulders during the dive, so the twist of the body does not spiral and rotate over the back entry position and create a long entry into the water.

There is a blind spot for the diver between the first quarter turn, when the eyes are focused downward on the water, and the second quarter turn or twist, when the head rolls backward with the chin stretched backward and the diver looks for the water as in the back dive entry into the water. The diver should complete the half twist in time to see the water in the back position before the body enters the water. On entry, the chin is tucked in to complete the vertical line of the body during entry. The body is tensed and held straight during the entire dive.

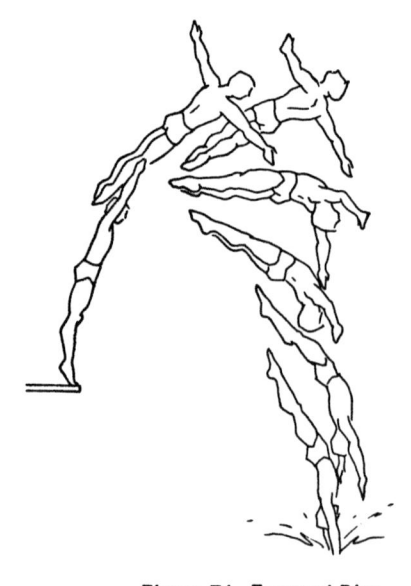

Figure 71. Forward Dive, One-Half Twist, Straight Position, Showing Take-Off, Arm Movement, One-Half Twist, and Head Placement Before the Second Quarter Turn, and Head Placement After the Twist Has Been Completed.

Forward Dive, One-Half Twist, Straight Position: What Can Go Wrong

Failure to Rotate on the Side Axis of the Body. Many beginning divers fail to twist the body from the forward position to the back position in the air. A common mistake is to try to keep the head and chin down when executing the twist. This has the effect of trying to turn a corner in the air. This will result in confusing the feeling of the dive more probably than an actual slap on the water. If this occurs, it is best to return to the dry land practice of the dive.

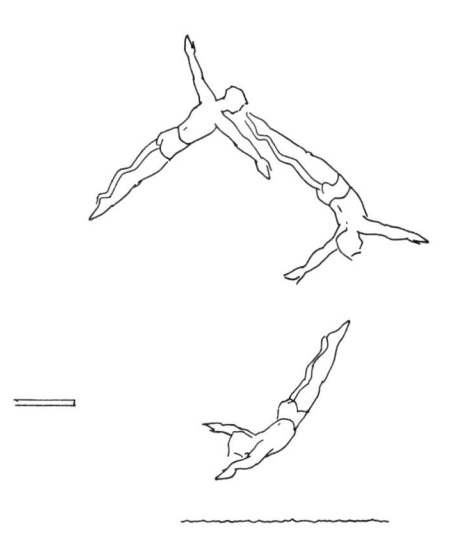

Figure 72. Failure to Rotate on the Side Axis of the Body in the Forward Dive, One-Half Twist, Straight Position.

Twisting from the Board. In their anxiety to complete the twist, beginning divers tend to start the body twist before they have left the board on the forward take-off. The twist is then initiated from the feet and knees and continues through the hips and shoulders instead of the opposite with the feet trailing the twist. This usually causes a long entry into the water and has the same effect as kicking the feet off the board before the straight body take-off has been completed.

Figure 73. Twisting from the Board in the Forward Dive, One-Half Twist, Straight Position.

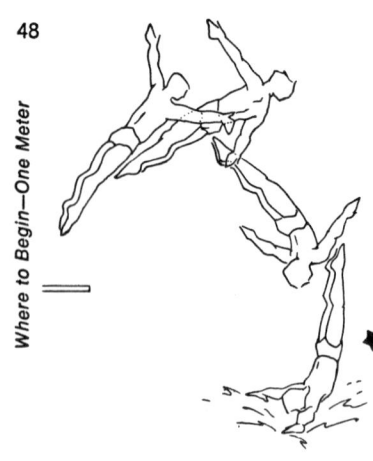

Figure 74. Pulling the Arms Too Low on the Sideward Swing or Lowering in the Forward Dive, One-Half Twist, Straight Position.

Pulling the Arms Too Low on the Sideward Swing or Lowering. As the arms are lowered sideward from the upward position, they should not drop below the horizontal position. If the arms are dropped lower than shoulder height, the body will overarch and that may cause a short entry into the water.

♣ **Saving the Forward Dive, One-Half Twist, Straight Position**

Short Entry. A short entry in the forward dive, one-half twist is a combination of a short back dive and a half twist that has not been completed. The slap is usually felt along the side of the body and legs. Keeping the body stretched as straight as possible and the chin tucked in will help to pull the dive to the correct angle of entry, even though it will not complete the twist.

Long Entry. The long entry on the forward dive, one-half twist, is a result of the legs traveling too far over the head during the dive. The effect is similar to the long entry on the back dive. Keep chin tucked in as far as possible for the entry into the water and allow the stretched body to spoon in forward to a shallow dive.

3a. Forward Dive, Pike Position

The forward dive in the pike position is introduced after the three dives presented in the straight position because it involves an additional body movement in the air as well as a different arm pattern. The forward dive in the pike position will later provide the diver with the fundamentals and the feeling of the inward dive from the back approach position. It is assumed that the diver can perform a close pike position and has enough strength in his lower back to be able to press the legs back to the straight position without the legs and hips becoming loose and wobbly.

Dry Land Practice

Stand on the pool deck with both feet together and the knees held straight. The arms are straight and down along the sides of the body. Swing both straight arms forward and upward, keeping the chin tucked in line with the spine. Bring both arms forward and downward, and lift one straight leg forward. Grasp the back of the leg with both hands. The chin stretches forward in this pike position and the eye focus is downward on the pool deck. Release the leg and swing both arms forward and upward while returning the lifted leg to the standing position. Tuck in the chin to simulate entry into the water.

From a Standing Position on the End of the Board

The diver should stand on the end of the board in the forward approach position and, without teetering the board or taking a bounce, swing both arms forward and upward to simulate take-off. Immediately bend at the hips, grasp the ankles with the hands (keeping the knees straight), and lift the chin so that the eyes can focus on the water in front of the board at the point of entry. Allow the body to fall off the board in this pike position, and when the weight of the body is off the feet, bring the arms forward and upward to the overhead position and tuck in the chin for entry into the water. When the body weight has left the board and the feet are free of the board, the legs are pressed upward to place the body in the vertical position for entry.

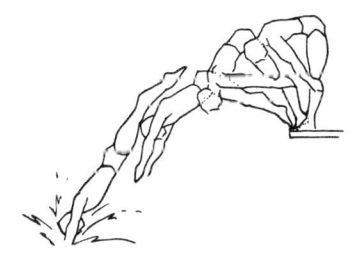

Figure 75. Forward Dive, Pike Position, Falling Off The Board.

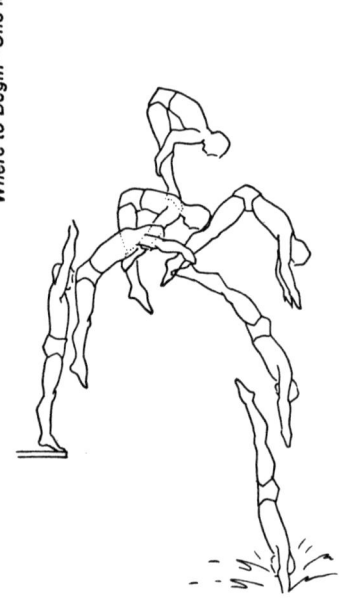

Figure 76. Forward Dive, Pike Position, Showing Take-Off, Pike Position at the Top of the Dive, Arm and Head Position, and Body Position During Entry.

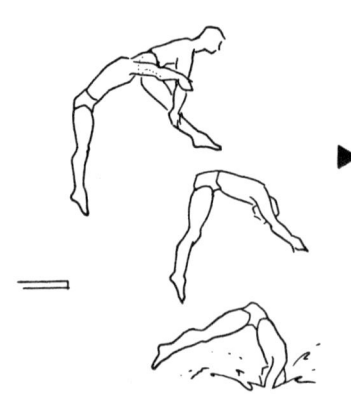

Figure 77. Failure to Lower the Shoulders in the Pike Position in the Forward Dive, Pike Position.

Forward Dive, Pike Position, from the Forward Approach

Next, proceed to the board and execute a forward dive in the pike position with the forward approach and slight lift-off from the board. The lift of the board is basically co-ordinated with the straight body position on take-off, but immediately after take-off the body bends at the hips and the arms reach forward and downward to grasp the back of the lower legs. The head is held upward in the pike position with the eye focus on the water at the point of entry. After the top of the body lift, when the downward motion of the body is felt, the legs are released and pressed upward for the straight body position. The arms swing forward to the overhead position, and the chin is tucked in for the entry into the water. The closed pike position is generally used for this dive.

As the diver gains experience in the take-off, performed in a straight body position, to the pike position in the air, to the straight body position for entry, he may employ his maximum lift from the board on the forward approach.

Control of the pike position is achieved by lowering the shoulders approximately parallel to the knees at the top of the dive.

Forward Dive, Pike Position: ▶ What Can Go Wrong

Failure to Lower the Shoulders in the Pike Position. This will cause the pike position in the air to face outward from the board instead of facing the water. It will result in a short entry or necessitate that the diver bend his knees to save the dive from a flat entry.

Kicking the Legs Overhead Before the Entry into the Water. When the legs are released by the hands in the pike position, the legs should press upward, not kick or swing vigorously overhead. This will cause an overarch of the back and possible long entry.

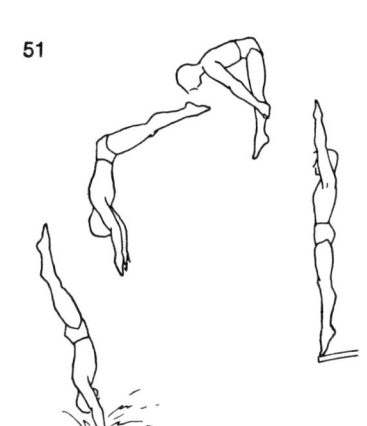

Figure 78. Kicking the Legs Overhead Before the Entry into the Water in the Forward Dive, Pike Position.

Failure to Lift Off the Board with Straight Body Before Assuming the Pike Position. This has the same effect as leaning the shoulders out over the water in the forward dive take-off. The knees must be completely straightened on take-off before any body position is assumed in the dive. The result is usually a drift of the body back toward the board, as well as a long entry into the water, which is difficult to save.

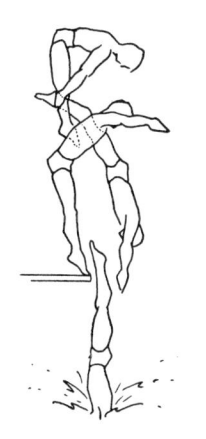

Figure 79. Failure to Lift Off the Board with Straight Body Before Performing the Pike Position in the Forward Dive, Pike Position.

♣ Saving the Forward Dive, Pike Position

Short Entry. A short entry on the forward dive in the pike position occurs when the diver's shoulders have not been tilted toward the water, and it becomes impossible for the diver to lift the legs upward for the entry position. The diver should tuck the chin in as far as possible and pull the bent knees up to the chest for the entry into the water. In this way, only the shins and feet will slap the water.

Long Entry. Many beginning divers are unable to keep the lower back and hips tensed in a dive that requires the body to progress from the bent hip position to the straight position. They may kick or swing the legs vigorously over the head for the forward entry position. This will create an overarch of the back and a long entry into the water. If this occurs, the diver should keep his chin stretched forward and outward until the hands go through the water in the entry, and immediately pull the chin down, bend at the hips, and roll forward in the water as the body passes through the water. The forward roll is executed below the surface of the water. Rolling the body too soon or above the water will cause a slap of the water on the back. The elbows should bend and the arms should be kept in front of the face to protect the face from a slap on the water.

4. Inward Dive, Pike Position

The inward dive in the pike position is similar to the forward dive in the pike position, with the exception that the inward dive begins from the back approach position on the board. The lift-off is different in that the hips stay in back of the shoulders on the take-off. The forward dive in the pike position should be under control before attempting the inward dive in the pike position.

Dry Land Practice

The dry land practice for the inward dive in the pike position is the same as that for the forward dive in the pike position, with the exception that the hips are in back of the shoulders on take-off and the head placement in the pike position is different. When the arms swing downward to grasp the one lifted leg, the head is pulled downward with the chin tucked. Since a forward body motion is performed from a back approach and take-off for the inward dive, the chin is tucked in during the pike in the air to help the shoulders tilt toward the water for the entry.

From a Standing Position on the End of the Board

Stand on the end of the board in the back approach position and swing the arms forward and upward, keeping the shoulders slightly in front of the hips. Bend the knees,

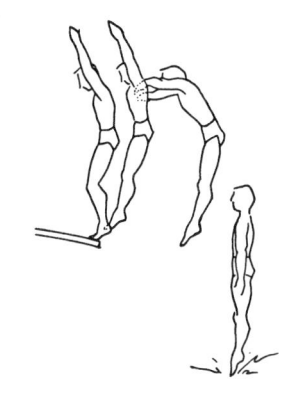

Figure 80. Jumping Off the Board Backward in Preparation for the Inward Dive, Pike Position.

Figure 81. Inward Dive, Pike Position, Showing Lift-Off, Pike Position, Head Placement, Arm Movement, and Entry into the Water.

and straighten the knees, lift the heels, and jump off the board backward, keeping the body in a slightly piked position to a feet-first entry into the water. There should be no shoulder lean backward on the take-off. The diver should be able to jump backward into the water in this position to a feet-first entry and clear the end of the diving board by at least three feet. Repeat the jump backward off the board several times, so that the diver can maintain a slightly piked position of the body with the arms held upward in the air and then placed along the sides of the body for the entry.

Inward Dive, Pike Position from the Backward Approach

Only after the forward dive in the pike position is under control, and the jump backward off the board in the pike position is consistent, should the diver proceed to the inward dive in the pike position with a take-off from the backward approach. The back approach take-off is executed with the knees straight and the hips slightly in back of the shoulders. When the arms swing forward and upward for the take-off and close to the sides of the head, the knees straighten and the toes press against the board for take-off. Immediately pull the arms and shoulders forward and downward and grasp the backs of the legs between the knees and ankles. Beginning divers should now tuck in the chin so as to help with the forward rotation of the shoulders to tilt the body in towards the water for the entry. Be certain not to bend at the hips, or pull the shoulders forward until the legs have straightened on the take-off and the body has left the board. When the downward motion is felt after the top of the dive, the diver should release the legs, bring the arms forward and overhead for the entry, keep the chin in line with the body, and lift or press the legs upward in line with the body for the straight entry into the water.

Inward Dive, Pike Position: ▶ What Can Go Wrong

Bending the Body at the Hips Before Take-Off from the Board. This will create a dangerous situation, causing the head and shoulders to lean forward too close to the board. The early bend of the hips may produce an over-rotation of the body in the pike position and may cause the diver to scrape his heels against the end of the board when he lifts his legs for the entry position.

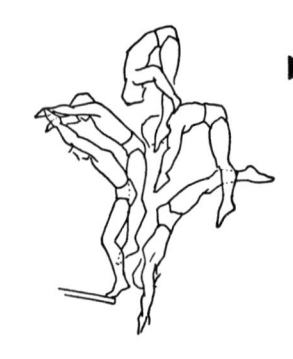

Figure 82. Bending the Body at the Hips Before Take-Off from the Board in the Inward Dive, Pike Position.

Failure to Lower the Shoulders to a Position Approximately Parallel to the Knees in the Pike Position. This error, as well as pulling the legs forward for the pike position instead of lowering the shoulders, will create a short entry or cause the diver to be unable to lift the legs high enough for the straight body position during entry into the water.

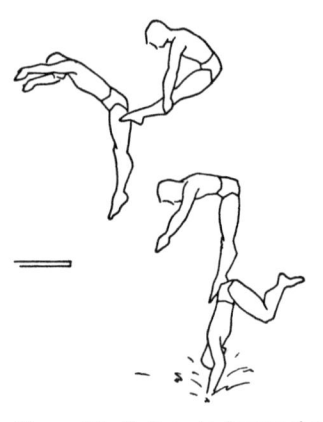

Figure 83. Failure to Lower the Shoulders to a Position Approximately Parallel to the Knees in the Pike Position on the Inward Dive, Pike Position.

Driving the Hips and Body Too Far Backward Off the Board During Take-Off. This will also hamper the diver's ability to tilt the shoulders forward toward the water for the straight entry, and will result in a short entry into the water.

Figure 84. Driving the Hips and Body Too Far Backward Off the Board During Take-Off in the Inward Dive, Pike Position.

♣ Saving the Inward Dive, Pike Position

Short Entry. In the inward dive, the lift-off height is not usually as great as that of the forward dive, and a short entry will not generally result in a slap of any force on the water, nevertheless, a short entry should be avoided if possible. If the diver cannot tilt completely forward for the entry into the water, he should pull the chin in as far as possible, bend the knees, and pull them to the chest for a tuck position entry into the water.

Long Entry. If the take-off from the board is properly timed, a long entry should not occur in the inward dive, pike position. The diver should be in control of the press of the legs upward for the entry before attempting the dive. A long entry may cause the backs of the heels to hit the board. Relax the knees immediately and bend at the hips as the body passes through the water.

4a. Inward Dive, Straight Position

The inward dive in the straight position requires more strength and tension of the body and a slightly higher lift-off from the board than the inward dive in the pike position. The take-off is the same as for the inward dive in the pike position, but instead of bending sharply at the hips to reach the pike position, the back remains straight, the arms lower sideward as in the forward dive in the straight position, the chin remains tucked in for the entire dive, and the shoulders tilt forward toward the entry point. After the feet leave the board, the straight legs lift backward and upward to create a pivot point for the straight body at the top of the dive. The body holds the straight position, with the arms sideward and the palms of the hands facing downward until the downward motion is felt. The arms are then lifted overhead for the straight entry position into the water.

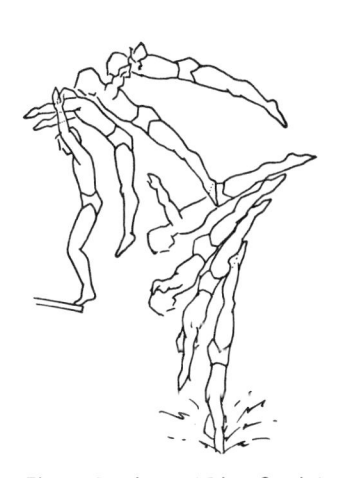

Figure 85. Inward Dive, Straight Position, Showing Take-Off, Straight Body Position, Arm and Head Placement, and Entry into the Water.

Beginning divers should proceed from the inward dive in the pike position to the straight position by widening the pike on each attempt and lifting the legs immediately after the feet leave the board.

5. Reverse Dive, Straight Position

The reverse dive in the straight position is introduced before the reverse dive in the tuck or pike position because the beginning diver must be able to take-off far enough away from the board for safety. In doing the reverse dive in the tuck or pike position, the beginning diver may accidentally lean back toward the board. The reverse dive in the straight position may create a short entry for the beginning diver, but errors in take-off are minimized. The body is not as likely to drift back toward the board in the straight body position take-off.

Dry Land Practice

Stand on the pool deck with the knees straight, the feet together, and the arms down at the sides of the body. Swing the straight arms forward and upward to simulate take-off and immediately press the hips forward in front of the shoulders in the standing position. Keep the heels on the pool deck. This will create a slight body arch but the chin remains in line with the spine and the eye focus is downward on the pool deck. The arms then are lowered sideward with the palms of the hands facing upward, and the chin is stretched back to simulate the position at the top of the dive. The shoulders and arms press backward with more force than in the back dive, and the chin extends backward as far as possible.

Jumping from the Forward Approach

Begin with the forward approach and take-off with a maximum lift off the board. When the

Figure 86. Forward Approach Jump-In in Preparation for the Reverse Dive, Straight Position.

feet press against the board for take-off, immediately press the hips forward to the slightly arched position and keep the arms upward and close to the sides of the head for the feet-first entry into the water. The chin remains tucked in during the jumping entry to avoid any backward rotation of the body. On the jumping tries into the water, the body should travel upward and outward away from the board approximately the same distance on each try. Consistency of take-off and body tightness are essential.

On the jump-in entry for the practice reverse position, the body is leaning backward. Separate the legs for the entry (one forward, and one backward) and bend slightly at the hips to avoid a back slap on the water.

Reverse Dive, Straight Position, from the Forward Approach

When the diver is able to take a forward approach with good consistency, jump feet first into the water with the body arched slightly and completely tensed, and is able to demonstrate the arm pull and hip snap on dry land, he may proceed to perform the reverse dive in the straight position from a forward approach and take-off from the board. It is not wise to cut down the lift from the board for the first attempt at the reverse dive. It is assumed that a fair amount of board control is possessed by the diver at this point in his diving experience to guarantee an unhurried take-off. The diver should be certain not to rush into the arched-back position before he has straightened his knees on the take-off from the board. On the take-off, the knees are straightened quickly as the feet press downward against the board. The hips are immediately pressed forward in front of the shoulders to the arched-back position as the arms are lowered sideward and the chin stretches backward so the diver is able to see the water for the downward motion of the body and

Figure 87. Reverse Dive, Straight Position, Showing Take-Off, Arm Position and Chin Extension at the Top of the Dive, and Arm and Body Position for Entry into the Water.

entry into the water. The chin does not extend backward until the body has completely left the board, with the knees straight and the body slightly arched. The knees are held straight and the toes are pointed. When the diver feels the downward motion of the body and can see the water at the point of entry, the arms are lifted directly overhead, the chin is tucked in line with the spine, and the body remains in the straight position for entry into the water.

Reverse Dive, Straight Position: ▶ What Can Go Wrong

Failure to Press the Hips Forward on Take-Off. This will prevent the shoulders from rotating backward. The legs will drop lower at top of the dive and the entry will be short.

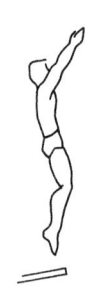

Figure 88. Failure to Press the Hips Forward on Take-Off in the Reverse Dive, Straight Position.

Failure to Straighten the Knees Completely Before Take-Off from the Board. If the knees do not completely straighten on the take-off from the board, the feet will skitter or slip off the board and the body will be projected forward instead of upward and forward off the board. A short entry will result, and possible drift back toward the board.

Figure 89. Failure to Straighten the Knees Completely Before Take-Off from the Board in the Reverse Dive, Straight Position.

Extending the Chin Backward Before Take-Off. This will rock the body back toward the board and can create a long entry.

★ Saving the Reverse Dive, Straight Position

Short Entry. If the reverse dive in the straight position is going to be short on the entry into the water, it is best for the diver to continue stretching the body and chin and to place the bent arms around the head to protect the face on the entry. If the chin is tucked in as for a vertical entry, it may flatten the dive and cause the back to slap on the water. Tucking in the chin on a short entry

Figure 90. Extending the Chin Backward Before Take-Off in the Reverse Dive, Straight Position.

will also hamper any opportunity of pulling the dive into the proper entry position. The chin should be extended backward as long as possible but once the body begins to pass through the water for the short entry, the chin is tucked in and the body bends at the hips to perform a shallow forward roll just under the surface of the water.

If the diver feels the downward motion of the reverse dive and still cannot see the water for the entry, he may bend his knees slightly and immediately kick the feet to straighten the knees, which will help to rotate the body to the proper entry position. If the diver makes several short entries on the reverse dive, he should return to the jump-in practice off the board and the preceeding dives until he has gained more diving experience.

Long Entry. On the long entry in the reverse dive in the straight position, the diver can usually see the water before entry but cannot stop the backward rotation of the body. He should tuck in the chin as far down as possible, keep the extended body position, and try to spoon forward into the water. If the body is rotating backward with greater acceleration, and the diver is high enough from the water, he may bend his knees to the tuck position and complete a somersault to a feet-first entry into the water.

INTERMEDIATE DIVES, ONE METER: OPTIONAL LIST

6. Forward Dive, One Somersault, Tuck Position

Single somersault dives are concluded with a feet-first entry into the water. The kinesthetic feeling of the forward somersault can best be introduced by pushing off in the water in a prone floating position with the arms extended overhead. Pull the arms, shoulders and head downward in the water and bend the knees in the tuck position. Grasp the shins with the hands and pull the tuck in as close as possible with the knees close to the shoulders. The diver should hold the tuck position in the water until he completes a full somersault forward and floats back to the prone position in the water. Performing a front somersault in the tuck position in the water will hamper the speed of the somersault, but the diver should have enough muscular quickness to push off from the wall and complete one somersault while floating in the water. This slow motion forward somersault will help the diver feel the rotation forward and allow him to practice the tight tuck position with the head down and without allowing the knees to slip away from the shoulders during the somersault. Any fault in the forward somersault in the tuck position can be detected before the diver attempts the somersault from the board.

Dry Land Practice

Stand with the legs straight, the feet together, and the arms down at the sides of the body. Swing both arms forward and upward to simulate take-off from the board. Swing the straight arms downward and bend at the hips so that the shoulders are almost touching the legs. Bend one knee, without bringing the leg forward, and grasp the one leg with both hands to pull the shoulder close to the knee. The head is down with the chin tucked as far downward as possible. Release the leg with the hands and stand upright with the chin tucked, and the straight arms at the sides of the body.

From a Standing Position on the End of the Board

Next, the diver may stand on the end of the board facing forward in the squat stand position with the hands grasping the shins be-

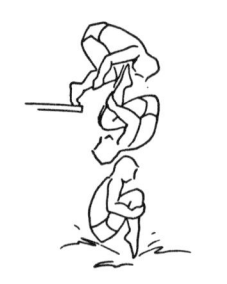

Figure 91. Forward Dive, One Somersault, Falling Forward from the Board.

tween the ankles and the knees. Pull the chin downward against the chest and roll forward from the diving board holding the tuck position. The entry will be in the sitting position into the water.

Forward Somersault, Tuck Position, from the Forward Approach

When the diver has completed the previously explained practice steps for the forward dive with one somersault, he may execute a forward approach and perform the somersault dive. Since the diver cannot see the water before the entry, he may spin too slowly or too fast on the first attempt. Judgment on the part of the diver as to when to release the tuck and extend the body in preparation for the entry will develop quickly after the first few attempts at the dive.

After take-off from the board, the arms swing downward, the shoulders pull forward and downward, and the hands grasp the shins. Do not bring the bent legs up to the shoulders. The knees bend for the tuck position after the hips have been bent and the upper body is leaning downward. Keep the chin down for the entire somersault. When the diver can see the water some distance in front of him, or the other end of the pool, he should release the legs from the tuck position and extend the body to the straight position with the arms down at the sides of the body for the entry into the water. The chin remains in line with the body for entry.

▶ Forward Dive, One Somersault, Tuck Position: What Can Go Wrong

Failure to Keep a Close Tuck Position During the Somersault Spin. If the knees slip away from the shoulders during the somersault, the forward rotation of the body will be stopped, causing a short entry into the water.

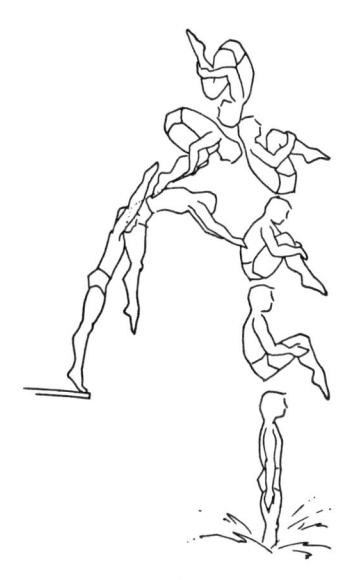

Figure 92. Forward Dive, One Somersault, Tuck Position, Showing Take-Off, Tuck Position at the Top of the Dive, Head and Arm Placement, and Body Extension for the Feet-First Entry into the Water.

Figure 93. Failure to Keep a Close Tuck Position During the Somersault in the Forward Dive, One Somersault, Tuck Position.

Figure 94. Failure to Release the Legs for the Entry (Overspin) in the Forward Dive, One Somersault, Tuck Position.

Figure 95. Failure to Extend the Body Fully at Take-Off Before Bending for the Tuck Position in the Forward Dive, One Somersault, Tuck Position.

Failure to Release the Legs for the Entry (Overspin). This is due to lack of experience in the feeling of the somersault. Usually the diver can see a quick flash of light as he is coming around the top of the somersault. If experience is lacking in the somersault feeling, the diver may not release the legs at that time and overspin the somersault to a long entry into the water.

Failure to Extend the Body Fully at Take-Off Before Bending for the Tuck Position. As with any dive, failing to wait for the complete extension of the body on take-off may result in a drift back in toward the board during the dive. It will also cause a short or long entry into the water, depending on the speed of the somersault.

★ **Saving the Forward Dive, One Somersault, Tuck Position**

Short Entry. If a short entry occurs, the diver will hit the water on his back. If the diver has released his legs too soon or has allowed his knees to slip away from his shoulders during the somersault, he should return to dry land practice and floating somersault in the water. If more than one short entry occurs, return to fundamental dives.

Long Entry. A long entry occurs when the diver folds into the tuck position too soon after take-off from the board or fails to release his legs upon completion of the somersault. If the diver can see the water at the point of entry and is still in the tuck position, he may keep the head tucked down and extend the arms overhead to protect the face on entry into the water. If the overspin of the somersault is slight, he may extend the body and lean backward with the shoulders and head, and extend one leg backward in a running position to splash into the water in a giant stride position.

7. Back Dive, One Somersault, Tuck Position

Once again, if the somersault backward has not been experienced, the diver should return to the water and push off the wall in a back floating position with the body extended and the arms extended overhead. The hips should be in line with the body in the floating position. Pull the bent knees up to the chest, extend the head backward in the water, grasp the shins with the hands and spin backward or somersault in the water until the back floating position is reached. Exhale through the nose to keep the water out of the nasal passages. This exercise will help the diver to feel the back somersaulting movement.

Dry Land Practice

Stand on the pool deck with the arms down at the sides of the body. Swing the arms forward and upward to simulate the back take-off. The chin remains tucked in line with the spine. The hips are slightly in front of the shoulders. Without bending the shoulders forward, lift one knee upward to the chest and grasp the shin with both hands, as the chin stretches backward. Release the leg to return to the standing position with the straight arms down at the sides of the body and the chin tucked in line with the body for the simulated entry position.

Back Dive, One Somersault, Tuck Position, from the Backward Approach

When the diver can perform a back somersault in the tuck position in the water from the floating position, and has good control of the backward approach and take-off, he may proceed to the back dive with one somersault in the tuck position from the board.

It is advisable to eliminate the back somersault from the standing position on the end of the board and proceed to the back somersault with a slight lift-off from the board. For the first few attempts, the beginning diver should lean out over the water a little more than the desired five-degree angle of take-off. In this way he will be guaranteed enough clearance from the end of the board. As experience is gained in the back somersaulting movement, the diver may resume the desired five-degree angle.

At the point of take-off, the body should be entirely extended with the arms overhead and the shoulders leaning backward slightly, with the head in line with the body. The knees are then bent and lifted to the chest, as the arms swing downward so that the hands may grasp the shins between the knees and ankles. As the knees are brought to the chest for the tuck position, the head drops backward slightly to initiate the somersault. The diver is usually able to see the water at the top of the lift of the dive when the body is in the tuck position. As the downward movement is felt by the diver, the hands release the legs and the body is stretched to the extended position for the feet-first entry into the water. Once the downward fall is begun, the chin pulls forward to the tucked position and remains in line with the body for the entry.

Figure 96. Back Dive, One Somersault, Tuck Position, Showing the Take-Off, Tuck Position of the Body, Arm and Head Placement and Entry into the Water.

Back Dive, One Somersault, Tuck Position: ▶ What Can Go Wrong

Failure to Extend the Body Completely on Take-Off. Sitting backward with the hips bent on the backward take-off may cause the feet to slip off the board and the body to drift in toward the board during the somersault. Many beginning divers are anxious to complete the back somersault and rush the take-off from the board. Sitting backward on the take-off may result in either a short or long entry because the spin and height of the somersault will be inconsistent.

Figure 97. Failure to Extend the Body Completely on the Back Take-Off in the Back Dive, One Somersault, Tuck Position.

Releasing the Legs Too Soon Before Entry. Diving experience will generally correct this fault, because the diver is able to see the water on the short entry.

Failure to Release the Legs After Completion of the Somersault. This will cause an overspin of the somersault and a subsequent long entry into the water.

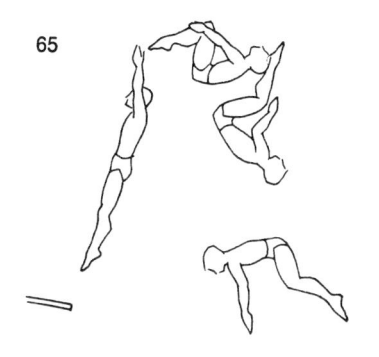

Figure 98. Releasing the Legs Too Soon Before Entry in the Back Dive, One Somersault, Tuck Position.

★ Saving the Back Dive, One Somersault, Tuck Position

Short Entry. A short entry or underspin of the somersault can be seen by the diver, and can be saved by pulling the bent knees to the chest to achieve the feet-first entry position into the water. If the entry is extremely flat, the diver should hold the bent arms in front of the face to save the face from the slap of the water.

Long Entry. If the body is still rotating backward when the hands release the legs for the entry into the water, the diver may continue rotating backward and slap the water with his back. If the diver can anticipate the long entry in the back somersault, he should immediately separate the legs to a stride (running) position and bend the knee of the lower leg. The back should be rounded and the arms held out to the side to absorb some of the force of the water.

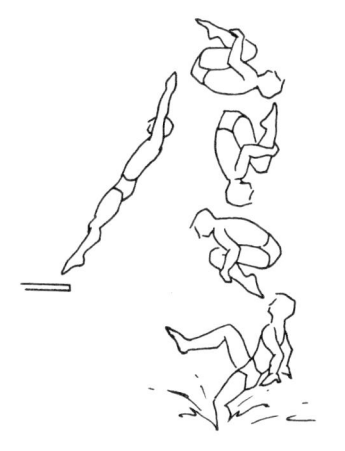

Figure 99. Failure to Release the Legs After Completion of the Somersault in the Back Dive, One Somersault, Tuck Position.

8. Forward Dive, One and One-Half Somersault, Tuck Position

The forward one and one-half somersault dive may follow the forward dive with one somersault, if the latter is in control and high enough above the water to allow time for an extended body entry into the water. The extra one-half somersault involves holding the body in the tuck position for a split second longer to place the body for the head-first entry.

Dry Land Practice

From the standing position on the pool deck, swing both arms forward and upward to simulate the take-off forward, and immediately swing the arms downward as the body bends at the hips and the shoulders lean forward close to the legs. Lift one leg with the knee bent and grasp the shin with both hands. The head is held down for the entire tuck position. The hands should continue to pull the bent legs as close to the chest as possible. Release the leg with the hands and immediately kick the leg straight and backward as the arms stretch overhead for the straight body entry position.

Forward Dive, One and One-Half Somersault, Tuck Position, from the Forward Approach

After successfully completing several forward dives with one somersault in the tuck position, proceed to the forward dive with one and one-half somersaults to the head-first entry into the water from the forward approach. The take-off should be consistent, with a complete body extension, but the hips should be slightly in back of the shoulders on take-off. The arms are fully extended on take-off with the hands slightly in back of the head. Bend at the hips and pull the arms, shoulders, and head down and forward first, before bending the knees to the tuck position. The diver should hold the tuck position with the chin down until he can see the water between his knees. After releasing the shins with the hands, kick the legs straight slightly below the vertical entry position, and swing the arms forward and overhead for the head-first entry into the water. When the hands

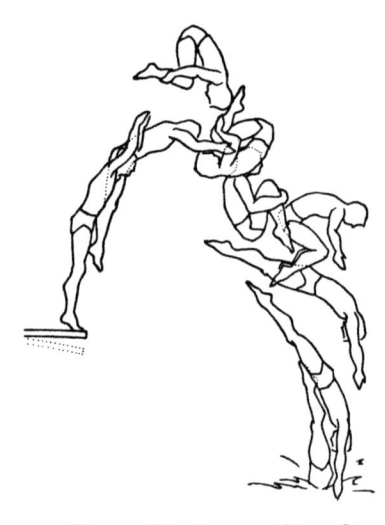

Figure 100. Forward Dive, One and One-Half Somersault, Tuck Position, Showing Take-Off, Tuck Position and Forward Spin at the Top of the Dive, Kick Out for Entry, and Head and Arm Placement.

release the legs, the eyes are focused downward on the water toward the point of entry. The chin is tucked in just before the entry into the water.

Forward Dive, One and One-Half Somersault, Tuck Position: ▶ What Can Go Wrong

Releasing the Legs Too Soon Before the Entry. This will result in a short entry even though the head may be in the proper position. Wait until the water is visible and the shoulders are tilted towards the water before releasing the legs.

Figure 101. Releasing the Legs Too Soon Before Entry in the Forward Dive, One and One-Half Somersault, Tuck Position.

Allowing the Head to Drift Backward During the Forward Somersault. This will slow down the somersault and result in a short entry.

Figure 102. Allowing the Head to Drift Backward During the Forward Somersault in the Forward Dive, One and One-Half Somersault, Tuck Position.

Bending the Body for the Tuck Position Before the Straight Body Take-Off. Again, as in any dive that is rushed from the board, this will cause the body to drift back toward the board during the dive. It will also cause a possible short entry into the water.

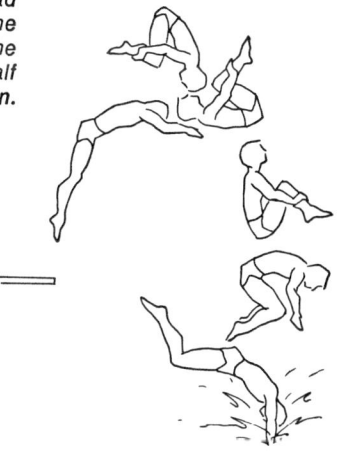

Figure 103. Bending the Body for the Tuck Position Before the Straight Body Take-Off in the Forward Dive, One and One-Half Somersault, Tuck Position.

★ **Saving the Forward Dive, One and One-Half Somersault, Tuck Position**

Short Entry. If the kick-out of the legs for the entry is too soon and the entry is going to be short, the diver should pull the head down as far as possible.

Long Entry. If the diver does not release the legs when the shoulders are tilted toward the water, or if he bends his head down for the entire dive and fails to see the water after the first somersault, he will experience a long entry and overarch of the back. If he kicks his legs over the hips on the entry, he will also experience an overarch of the back and long entry. The diver should return to the single somersault and dry land practice of the forward one and one-half somersault. The diver may want to execute a forward roll just under the surface of the water as his body passes through the water for the long entry to prevent straining of the muscles of the back.

8a. Forward Dive, One and One-Half Somersault, Pike Position

The pike position in the forward one and one-half somersault dive can be achieved with initial success if the same dive in the tuck position is in good control, and is high enough above the water for the extended body position entry into the water. Either the closed or open pike position may be employed for this dive. A fair degree of lower back and hip strength is necessary to prevent an overarch of the back when the legs lift overhead for the entry position.

9. Inward Dive, One Somersault, Tuck Position

The inward dive with one somersault in the tuck position may be attempted when the diver has gained control of the inward dive in the pike position and the forward somersault from the board. He should be at least three feet from the end of the board when his body enters the water in the inward dive in the pike position before progressing to the inward somersault.

Dry Land Practice

From the standing position on the pool deck with both feet together and the legs straight, swing both arms forward and upward, close to the sides of the head. Immediately swing the arms forward and downward, pull the chin downward and bend the body forward. Lift one knee and grasp the shin of the lifted leg with the hands and pull the leg as close to the chest as possible. Release the leg with the hands and lower the arms to the sides of the body as the leg is lowered to the standing position, to simulate the feet-first entry into the water. The chin is held down for the entire dive.

Inward Dive, One Somersault, Tuck Position, from a Backward Approach

The dive is initiated in the same manner as the inward dive in the pike position from the board. After the take-off from the board, the body is bent at the hips immediately and the shoulders lean forward. The arms swing downward and forward to grasp the shins and pull the legs close to the chest for the tuck position. Once the diver has left the board in the extended body position with the hips slightly in back of the shoulders, the body immediately bends and tucks for the spin of the somersault. Once the knees have been straightened for the take-off from the board, the chin is pulled downward as far as possible to help the body spin forward for the somersault. The take-off from the board should drive the body upward and backward with the hips in back of the shoulders.

Upon completion of the somersault, the diver is able to see the board in front of him. He then extends the legs to the straight position with the arms down at the sides for the feet-first entry. The head is lifted so that the chin is in line with the spine for the entry into the water.

The first few attempts at the inward somersault dive may result in a short entry into the water, with the diver hitting the water in the sitting position. This is to be expected, as the beginning diver will push the dive too far backward off the board, to guarantee enough clearance from the board for the somersault. When more experience has been gained in lifting the body upward for the inward somersault, the diver will be able to achieve greater height from the board with less backward push. The spin of the somersault forward from the back lift-off is also hampered when the body is pushed too far backward from the board. However, if the entries are still extremely short after several attempts of the inward somersault the diver should return to the forward dive with one somersault and the inward dive in the pike position until greater control of the somersault and lift off the board has been achieved.

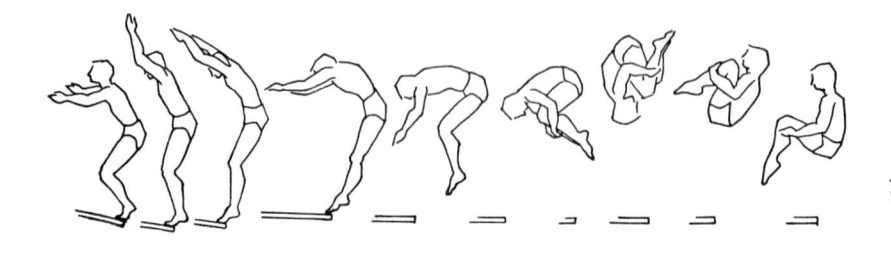

Figure 104. Inward Dive, One Somersault, Tuck Position, Showing Take-Off, Tuck Position at the Top of the Dive, Head and Arm Placement and Entry into the Water.

Figure 105. Bringing the Knees Forward to the Shoulders in the Inward Dive, One Somersault, Tuck Position.

Inward Dive, One Somersault, Tuck Position: ▶ What Can Go Wrong

Bringing the Knees Forward to the Shoulders. The shoulders should lean forward and downward to the legs before the diver grabs the shins for the tuck position. Bringing the bent knees forward after take-off will slow the forward spin of the somersault and cause a short entry.

Failure to Keep the Tuck Position. This may cause not only a short entry but a possible slap of the back on the water. Once the body has left the board, the tuck position should be held as tight as possible.

Figure 106. Failure to Keep the Tuck Position in the Inward Dive, One Somersault, Tuck Position.

Pushing Too Far Backward on Take-Off. This will cause a slow body rotation in the somersault and a short entry into the water.

Figure 107. Pushing Too Far Backward on Take-Off in the Inward Dive, One Somersault, Tuck Position.

Bending the Hips for the Somersault Before the Knees Have Straightened for the Take-Off. This is a dangerous error that will cause the body to drift toward the board during the dive. The diver should be certain to wait for the entire take-off sequence before performing any part of the dive.

★ Saving the Inward Dive, One Somersault, Tuck Position

Figure 108. Bending for the Somersault Before the Knees have Straightened for the Take-Off in the Inward Dive, One Somersault, Tuck Position.

Short Entry. In a short entry, the diver usually hits the back or back of the hips on the water. It is best to keep the tuck position as tight as possible and the chin digging downward as much as possible to try and save the dive.

Long Entry. The long entry on the inward dive with one somersault does not occur often, because the diver is able to see the board as his body has completed the somersault and he is falling downward for the entry. If he fails to release his legs at that time, he will overspin the somersault and slap face first on the water. The diver should extend his arms forward and slap the water with his hands and try to lean the shoulders backward to save the long entry.

10. Reverse Dive, One Somersault, Tuck Position

The reverse dive with one somersault in the tuck position may be attempted after the back somersault has been achieved with good control, and the forward approach is consistent. The beginning diver may find the reverse somersault dive easier to achieve than the reverse dive in the straight position.

Dry Land Practice

From a standing position on the pool deck with the knees straight and the feet together, swing both arms forward and upward to simulate take-off with the hips pressed slightly in front of the shoulders. Drop the head backward and bring the arms forward and downward, as one knee is lifted so the hands can grasp the bent leg at the shin and pull it close to the chest in the tuck position. Release the leg and return to the standing position. Lower the arms to the sides of the body and tuck in the chin to simulate the feet-first entry into the water.

Reverse Dive, One Somersault, Tuck Position, from the Forward Approach

The take-off from the board is in the extended

body position with the hips slightly in front of the shoulders. The arms are held upward and close to the sides of the head. After leaving the board, the head is dropped backward and the knees are bent and lifted to the chest. The arms swing downward and the hands grasp the shins to pull the body into the tuck position. When the diver can see the water backward, and his shoulders and knees are approximately horizontal to the water, and level to each other, he should release the legs, lower the arms, and extend the body for the feet-first entry into the water.

For the first few attempts at the reverse dive with one somersault in the tuck position, the diver should lean slightly forward from the usual five-degree angle of take-off so he may ascertain his position from the board. The knees should straighten completely on take-off with the hips slightly in front of the shoulders. Adjustments will have to be made by the diver as to when to release the legs in preparation for entry, depending on the height of the dive and the speed of the somersault. Releasing the legs will stop the spin of the somersault. When experience has been gained in the reverse somersault, the diver may reduce the forward lean from the board on take-off and extend the body to the five-degree angle of take-off.

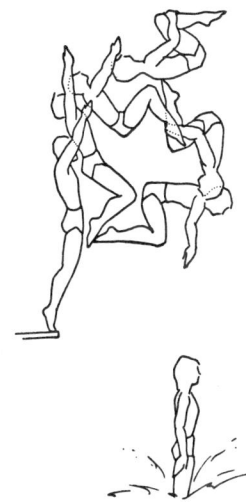

Figure 109. Reverse Dive, One Somersault, Tuck Position, Showing the Take-Off, Tuck Position at the Top of the Dive, Arm and Head Placement, and Entry into the Water.

Reverse Dive, One Somersault, Tuck Position: What Can Go Wrong

Failure to Straighten the Knees and Press the Hips Forward on Take-Off. The knees should be completely straightened on take-off for the reverse somersault dive, with the hips pressed forward. Failure to straighten the knees will result in the feet slipping off the board instead of pressing downward against the board for the take-off. The somersault will be incomplete, and the body will travel out forward from the board, resulting in a short entry.

Figure 110. Failure to Straighten the Knees on Take-Off in the Reverse Dive, One Somersault, Tuck Position.

Dropping the Head Backward Too Soon Before Take-Off. This will result in a drift toward the board during the dive. It is a serious error and must be avoided.

Figure 111. Dropping the Head Backward Too Soon Before Take-Off in the Reverse Dive, One Somersault, Tuck Position.

Releasing the Tuck Position Too Soon. Releasing the tuck position before the body is at least horizontal to the water stops the completion of the somersault and results in a short entry.

Figure 112. Releasing the Tuck Position Too Soon in the Reverse Dive, One Somersault, Tuck Position.

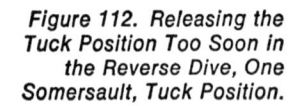

Figure 113. Releasing the Tuck Position Too Late in the Reverse Dive, One Somersault, Tuck Position.

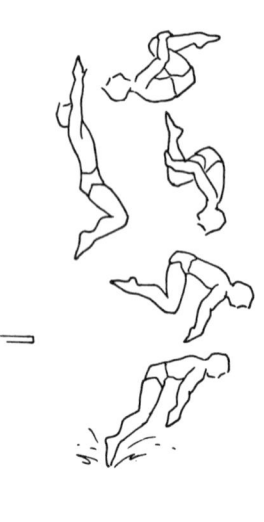

Releasing the Tuck Position Too Late. Holding the tuck position beyond the vertical position will result in a long entry with the back slapping the water.

★ **Saving the Reverse Dive, One Somersault, Tuck Position**

Short Entry. The short entry is an incomplete somersault with the body hitting the water forward in the tuck position or the horizontal body position. Place the hands and forearms in front of the face, pull in the chin as far as possible and keep the knees in the tuck position.

Long Entry. Failure to release the tuck position in time will result in a continuation of the somersault to a long entry into the water, with the body hitting the water on the back. Keep the chin in and swing the arms sideward and backward so they hit the water first. The diver should separate the legs into the running position and round the back so that he may execute a giant stride with a lean backward into the water.

11. Forward Dive, One and One-Half Somersault, One-Half Twist, Tuck Position

When the diver has good control of the forward dive with one and one-half somersaults in the tuck position and is able to release the tuck position when his body is still above board height, he is ready to add a one-half twist of the body to the back entry position into the water.

Dry Land Practice

Stand on the pool deck with both legs straight and the arms down at the sides of the body. Swing both arms forward and upward to simulate take-off from the board. Bring the arms forward and downward as one leg is bent and brought forward for the tuck position. Both hands grasp the shin of the lifted leg to simulate the one and one-half somersault in the tuck position. The head is held down. Release the tuck and as the arms swing forward for the simulated entry, the released leg extends backwards so that the toe is touching the pool deck. Immediately roll the hips, shoulders, and head sideward as the arms extend sideward. Complete the half twist on the foot supporting the body weight and lift the arms overhead with the head first back and then tucked in for the back entry position. See Figure 5 and Figure 70 showing same positions on board.

Forward Dive, One and One-Half Somersault, One-Half Twist, Tuck Position, from the Forward Approach

Adding a half twist to the one and one-half somersault dive forward should be undertaken only when the one and one-half somersault and the forward half twist dives are understood and in good control, with enough height off the board to accomplish both. The one and one-half forward somersault is identical to that previously described, with the exception that the release of the legs from the tuck position before the entry is slightly earlier, to allow a horizontal extension of the body as the shoulders and hips initiate the half twist. On the release of the legs from the tuck position, the eye focus is downward on the water at the point of entry. When the body begins the half twist, the head rolls backward for the back entry position into the water. When the hands release the legs in the tuck position, the arms swing sideward for the half twist and immediately lift overhead for the back entry into the water.

Figure 114. Forward Dive, One and One-Half Somersault, One-Half Twist, Tuck Position, Showing the Take-Off, Tuck Position at the Top of the Dive, Kick Out and Body Extension for the Half Twist, and Back Entry into the Water.

Forward Dive, One and One-Half Somersault, One-Half Twist, Tuck Position: ▶ What Can Go Wrong

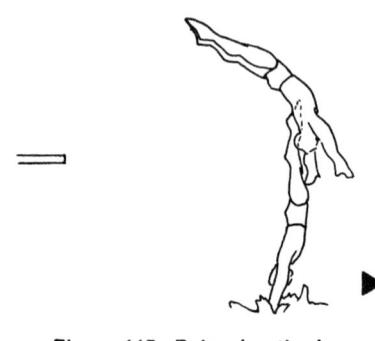

Figure 115. Releasing the Legs from the Tuck Position Too Late in the Forward Dive, One and One-Half Somersault, One-Half Twist, Tuck Position.

Releasing the Legs from the Tuck Position Too Late. Releasing the legs from the tuck position too late will cause a spiraling action of the body and a long entry on the half twist.

Releasing the Legs from the Tuck Position Too Soon. This will cause a short entry into the water which will slap the back and the back of the legs on entry.

Figure 116. Releasing the Legs from the Tuck Position Too Soon in the Forward Dive, One and One-Half Somersault, One-Half Twist, Tuck Position.

Failure to Complete the Half Twist. The body will enter the water sideward.

✤ Saving the Forward Dive, One and One-Half Somersault, One-Half Twist, Tuck Position

Short Entry. The short entry may be nothing more than failing to complete the entire half twist and going through the water facing sideways. But the short entry may cause a back slap if the half twist has been completed but the legs are as low as the shoulders and the body is not high enough above the water to complete the stretch for the entry. If this occurs, return to the one and one-half forward somersault dive without the half-twist until greater height from the board and body control has been achieved.

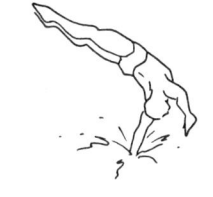

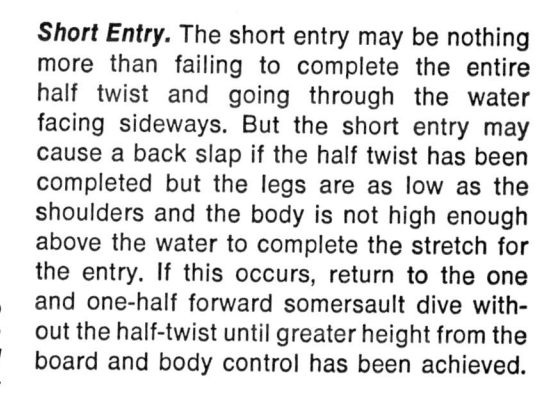

Figure 117. Failure to Complete the Half Twist in the Forward Dive, One and One-Half Somersault, One-Half Twist, Tuck Position.

Long Entry. The long entry may be saved by keeping the chin tucked and extending the body so the body may spoon forward into a shallow dive in the water.

WHERE TO BEGIN—
THREE METER

From the one-meter board, almost any kind of splashing entry into the water can be tolerated by the diver with only mild discomfort. But the story is entirely different from the three-meter board. The slightest deviation in body alignment, arm position, and head placement can result in muscle strain and a hard slap on the water. Dives and entries should be in good control from the one-meter board before employing them on the three-meter board. It is not advisable to begin the fundamentals of diving on the three-meter board without having first achieved success in the fundamentals from the one-meter board.

The forward and backward dry approach should also be practiced on the three-meter board with caution until sure-footedness has been gained. The fault of body relaxation going through the water during the entry must be eliminated before the diver proceeds to three-meter diving.

Contrary to the belief of beginning divers, there is not much more time in the air to complete the dive from three meters than from one meter. As in the case of the one-meter board, the dives must be essentially completed by the time the diver's body drops in the air to the board level. From either board height, once the body has dropped below the level of the board, the diver has only enough time to get set and stretch for the entry. For this reason many beginning divers float from the three-meter board, do not complete the dive, and hit the water with a short entry. A certain degree of experience in diving is necessary before the diver will want to proceed to the high board.

The diver may begin on the three-meter board with a feet-first entry by jumping off the board, and then perform a falling forward dive from a stand on the end of the board.

BEGINNING DIVES, THREE METER

1. Falling Forward Dive, Straight Position from a Stand on the End of the Board

Stand on the end of the board facing forward with the arms down at the sides of the body and the body held tense. The head should be held in line with the body. Fall forward in this tense body position, keeping the arms at the sides of the body. When the body has fallen to the horizontal position and the weight of the body has left the feet, swing the arms forward and upward and stretch for the entry into the water.

Figure 118. Falling Forward Dive, Straight Position from a Stand on the End of the Board.

2. Falling Back Dive, Straight Position, from a Stand on the End of the Board

Stand on the end of the board in the back approach position, with the arms at the sides of the body. The chin is held in and the head is in line with the body. The hips should be slightly in front of the shoulders. Begin falling backward, keeping the body tensed and the arms down at the sides of the body. The diver should lower the head backward so that he may see the water. When the body has fallen to the horizontal position, lift the arms overhead and tuck the chin for the back entry into the water.

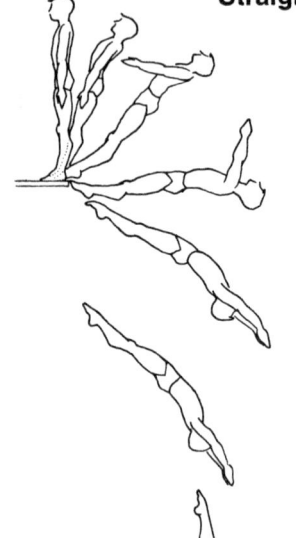

Figure 119. Falling Back Dive, Straight Position from a Stand on the End of the Board.

COMPLETING THE LIST, THREE METER

After the falling forward dive and the falling back dive from a stand are under control, the diver may proceed to the forward approach and attempt a forward dive with the lift of the three-meter board. Also proceed to the back dive from the back approach. These dives should be repeated many times, and the fulcrum should be adjusted forward or backward, so the diver may be correctly timed with the speed of the lift of the board. Repeating the forward and backward dives many times will allow the diver to correct any faults in the entry into the water. He will also feel the difference in falling time off the three-meter board. He will gain board experience and learn how to save the short and long entry in the forward and backward entries into the water.

When the diver has control of the falling time from the three-meter board and has a tensed straight body during the entry into the water, he may perform any dive from the three-meter board which he has mastered on the one-meter board. This mastery includes the following seven accomplishments:

1. He has ability to stand up on the take-off without excessive body lean.

2. He has good body control in the air. He is able to hold the tuck, pike, and straight positions. He is able to keep the knees straight and the back tight.

3. He has a good entry position, with the head in line with the spine.

4. He does not relax his body as he enters the water.

5. The diver has eliminated on the one-meter board the common faults of the take-off and dive that he is going to attempt from the three-meter board.

6. He is able to save the dive from the short or long entry.

7. He fully understands the mechanics of the dive he is going to perform and is able to concentrate on the dive.

Very young divers may not be able to control the entries into the water from the three-meter board. It is wise to continue learning to dive from the one-meter board until body tension is assured.

DRY LAND PRACTICE

Before each dive from the three-meter board, the dry land practice for that dive should be reviewed. The most experienced divers go through the motions of each dive on dry land before they proceed to the board.

OTHER AIDS IN LEARNING TO DIVE

TRAMPOLINE

Many divers bounce on the trampoline to improve footwork, leg strength, and body positions in diving.

Footwork

The bed of the trampoline affords much the same timing as the springboard and the diver is able to practice the dry approaches on the trampoline without the pounding of the hard surface of the board. Common faults of the steps and hurdle may be easily observed. Arm and leg coordination may be improved by practicing the forward dry approach from one end of the trampoline to the middle of the trampoline.

Body Positions

The body positions in diving (tuck, pike, and

straight) may be practiced on the trampoline by bouncing on the feet, assuming the body position on the upward lift from the trampoline, and then releasing the position and continue bouncing on the feet. Care should be taken to remain in the center of the trampoline while bouncing, with the eye focus downward on the bed at all times.

Leg Strength

Leg strength and body tightness may be improved with continuous bouncing on the trampoline, which is not possible on the diving board. When bouncing on the trampoline, the legs are held straight when the body is in the air and the knees bend only when contacting the trampoline with the feet. As with the diving board, the entire foot is placed on the trampoline before lifting off again for the next bounce.

Advanced skills on the trampoline, such as somersaults and somersaults with a twisting movement, should not be attempted without the use of an overhead suspension belt with a qualified teacher in attendance.

FILMS AND TAPES

Many schools have television cameras with tapes that instantly replay the performance of the diver. This is an extremely helpful aid to point out common faults. The diver is able to compare how the dive feels and how the dive looks at almost the same time.

In addition, many films on diving are available to show the diver championship form on the board, in the air, and during the entry. For the serious diver, a film may be taken of his list of dives each year to show improvement.

JACKETS

As the diver progresses to an untried dive, some teachers prefer to have the divers wear a jacket or shirt in case of slapping the water on the short or long entry into the water. Jackets of synthetic fiber which do not absorb the water are best for this use. The jacket should fit tightly to avoid becoming tangled around the diver's head under water. A general rule is to avoid jackets by continued dry land practice and diving progressions to guarantee success of the next dive. Any dive that is slapped more than two or three times should be avoided until more experience is attained on the board.

PRACTICE SESSIONS

The beginning diver should go through his entire list of dives at each practice session if possible, even though he is not seriously thinking about diving competition. In this way, he will gain more control of his footwork on the board and improve his awareness of the kinesthetic feeling of the different dives. The kinesthetic feeling of the dives and the timing of the board are quickly lost as time elapses between practice sessions. It is important at each practice session that a teacher or fellow diver observe the dives to point out how the dive looks and what is going wrong. A small flaw in execution may become a permanent habit if not detected and mentioned.

The length of the practice session should be determined by the diver's ability to concentrate on the dives and to avoid fatigue. Balking on a dive is a useful aid during the practice session when the diver feels there is something wrong with his steps or hurdle, but continuous balking indicates the diver is unable to concentrate on the dive or that he is tired.

Practice sessions usually begin with a dry land warm-up consisting of stretching and strengthening exercises on the pool deck, continue with dry approaches on the board, both forward and backward, and conclude with the performance of each dive on the list three or four times, beginning with the simple dives. Learning a new dive is usually introduced after the conclusion of the regular practice session. If the diver has a complete list of eleven dives he can perform on both boards, he may practice on the one-meter board in one practice session and on the three-meter board in another session. For the beginning diver, practice sessions may last from one-half hour to two hours in length, two or three days a week. No matter how anxious the diver may be to learn to dive, once he is tired physically and can no longer concentrate on the dive and instruction, his diving practice session should be concluded for that day.

A GOOD BEGINNING LIST FOR COMPETITION

The list of dives presented in Chapter 4 represents an adequate list for the diver who is interested in competition. The degree of difficulty for the optional dives presented is 9.8. The Amateur Athletic Union requires a list of eleven dives, including five required dives (one from each category) and six optional dives (one from each category and one additional dive of the diver's choice).

Most high school competitions require a list of six dives (one required dive and five optional dives from any category). Collegiate competitions usually require six dives for dual meets, and a complete list of eleven dives for district and national championship competitions. Age group competitions may require four, five, or six dives, depending on the age of the children.

WHAT THE JUDGES LOOK FOR IN A GOOD DIVE

Dives are rated from zero to ten in a competition. The judges do not judge the degree of difficulty of the dive, only the execution of the dive. A minimum of three judges are necessary because the three scores are added together and multiplied by the degree of difficulty of the dive to determine the total score for that dive. If five judges are present, the high score and the low score are dropped and the three middle scores are added and multiplied by the degree of difficulty of the dive for the score.

For example,

DIVE	JUDGE	SCORE FOR THE DIVE	TOTAL SCORE
Forward Dive, Straight Position	1	6.5 high score	
	2	4.0 low score	
Degree of Difficulty	3	5.0	
1.4	4	+ 5.5 + = 16.5 × 1.4	23.1
	5	6.0	

Recent rules state that only the dive itself is to be judged, not the approach or what happens when the diver is fully submerged under the water. The take-off, however, affects the dive.

Most judges look for the following:

1. Take-Off. Body fully extended with no more than five degree body lean off the board. The dive should not lean to one side of the board. The diver is able to depress the board and rise with the lift of the board. The legs are straight on take-off with the toes pointed.

2. Top. The execution of the dive is at the top of the lift from the board.

3. Body Positions. The diver is able to hold a close tuck or pike position with the toes pointed. The knees are held perfectly straight in the pike position. The diver is able to perform a straight position without an overarch of the body, with the toes pointed and the legs straight. The arms are directly upward when called for and directly sideward in the straight position dive. The arms must not drop below the horizontal position, remain higher than the horizontal position, or drop in back of the chest or in front of the chest away from the horizontal arm position. In the tuck position, the elbows should be held close to the legs, not protruding outward. The arms are held directly overhead for the head-first entry.

4. Entry. The body should be as close to the vertical position as possible and no more than five degrees from the vertical position for the entry into the water. The entry should be clean or soft, that is, without undue water splash. This is accomplished by a fully extended body with the arms overhead for the head-first entry and the arms at the sides of the body for the feet-first entry. The body should not be rotating or arched during the entry. The head should be in line with the spine, and the entry should be approximately two to three feet from the end of the board.

5. Style. In diving, style and correctness of execution are synonymous. Style emerges when control, height from the board, proper execution of the dive, correct timing of the top, and a vertical entry into the water have been achieved. The body should demonstrate a smoothness of motion during the dive. Any excessive jerking movement will detract from the artistry of the dive. The arms should be straight in straight-position dives, but hyperextension of the arms that will cause a stiff look to the dive is undesirable.

1 meter Springboard	3 meter Springboard	DEGREES OF DIFFICULTY	5 to 7.5 meter Platform	10 meter Platform
a b c d	a b c d	DIVE NUMBER / ORDER OF EXECUTION / FORWARD DIVES	a b c d	a b c d
1.4 1.2 1.2 —	1.6 1.3 1.3 —	101 Forward Dive	1.4 1.3 1.3 —	1.6 1.4 1.4 —
1.7 1.5 1.4 —	1.8 1.7 1.7 —	102 Fwd. somersault	1.7 1.5 1.5 —	1.9 1.7 1.7 —
— 1.7 1.6 —	— 2.1 1.6 1.6	103 Fwd. 1½ som.	— 1.5 1.4 —	2.0 1.6 1.5 —
— 2.2 2.0 —	— — 2.2 2.1	104 Fwd. Double som.	— 2.0 1.9 —	2.6 2.3 2.3 —
— 2.6 2.3 —	— — 2.3 2.1	105 Fwd. 2½ som.	— 2.3 1.9 —	— 2.2 2.0 —
— — 2.6 —	— — 2.7 2.5	106 Fwd. Triple som.	— — — —	— — — —
— — 3.0 —	— — 3.0 2.7	107 Fwd. 3½ som.	— — — —	— 2.9 2.6 —
1.7 1.5 — —	1.7 1.6 — —	112 Fwd. Flying som.	1.5 1.4 — —	1.8 1.7 — —
1.9 1.8 — —	1.8 1.7 — —	113 Fwd. Flying 1½ som.	1.7 1.6 — —	1.8 1.7 — —
— — — —	— — — —	114 Fwd. Flying Double som.	— — — —	— — 2.3 —
— — — —	— — — —	115 Fwd. Flying 2½ som.	— — — —	— — 2.4 —
— — — —	— — — —	116 Fwd. Som. with Flying 1½	— — — —	— — 2.5 —
		II · BACK DIVES		
1.6 1.6 1.6 —	1.7 1.7 1.7 —	201 Back Dive	1.6 1.6 1.6 —	1.9 1.9 1.8 —
1.7 1.6 1.5 —	1.6 1.7 1.5 —	202 Back Somersault	1.6 1.5 1.5 —	1.7 1.7 1.6 —
2.4 2.3 2.2 —	2.2 2.2 2.0 —	203 Back 1½ Som.	— 1.9 1.8 —	2.3 2.2 2.1 —
— 2.3 2.2 —	2.4 2.2 2.0 —	204 Back Double Som.	— 2.0 — —	— 2.3 2.2 —
— — — —	— 3.0 2.8 —	205 Back 2½ Som.	— — — —	— 2.9 2.6 —
1.8 1.7 — —	— 1.6 — —	212 Back Flying Som.	— 1.5 — —	— 1.7 — —
— — — —	— 2.1 — —	213 Back Flying 1½ Som.	— — — —	— 2.2 — —
		III · REVERSE DIVES		
1.7 1.7 1.7 —	1.9 1.9 1.7 —	301 Reverse Dive	1.7 1.6 1.6 —	2.0 2.0 1.8 —
2.0 1.8 1.6 —	1.9 1.7 1.5 —	302 Reverse Somersault	1.8 1.5 1.4 —	2.0 1.6 1.5 —
2.8 2.5 2.3 —	2.6 2.4 2.2 —	303 Reverse 1½ Som.	— 2.2 1.9 —	2.5 2.3 2.2 —
— 2.2 — —	— 2.4 2.2 —	304 Reverse Double Som.	— 2.0 — —	— 2.3 2.2 —
— — — —	— 3.0 2.8 —	305 Reverse 2½ Som.	— — — —	— — 2.7 —
1.8 1.7 — —	— 1.6 — —	312 Reverse Flying Som.	— 1.8 1.6 —	— 1.7 — —
— — — —	— 2.4 — —	313 Reverse Flying 1½ Som.	— — — —	— — 2.3 —
		IV · INWARD DIVES		
1.7 1.3 1.2 —	1.6 1.3 1.2 —	401 Inward Dive	1.5 1.3 1.1 —	1.6 1.4 1.3 —
1.9 1.7 — —	1.7 1.5 — —	402 Inward Somersault	1.6 1.5 — —	1.7 1.7 — —
2.4 2.2 — —	2.2 2.0 — —	403 Inward 1½ Som.	1.7 1.6 — —	1.8 1.6 — —
— 2.3 — —	2.4 2.3 — —	404 Inward Double Som.	— — — —	2.3 2.1 — —
— — — —	2.9 2.6 — —	405 Inward 2½ Som.	— — — —	2.7 2.4 — —
— — — —	— 1.8 — —	412 Inward Flying Som.	— — — —	— 1.8 — —
— — — —	— 2.3 — —	413 Inward Flying 1½ Som.	— — — —	— 2.0 — —
		V · TWIST DIVES		
1.8 1.7 — —	1.9 1.8 — —	5111 Fwd. Dive, ½ Twist	1.7 1.7 — —	1.9 1.9 — —
2.0 2.1 — —	2.0 2.1 — —	5112 Fwd. Dive, 1 Twist	1.8 — — —	2.0 — — —
— — 1.7 —	1.9 1.7 — —	5121 Fwd. Som. ½ Twist	— — — —	— — — —
— — 2.0 —	— — — 2.0	5122 Fwd. Som. 1 Twist	— — — —	— — — —
— — 2.2 —	— — — —	5124 Fwd. Som. 2 Twists	— — — —	— — — —
— 2.1 2.0 —	2.0 1.9 — —	5131 Fwd. 1½ Som. ½ Twist	— — — —	— — — —
— — 2.2 —	— — — 2.1	5132 Fwd. 1½ Som. 1 Twist	— — 2.0 —	— — — 2.1
— — 2.7 —	— — — 2.4	5134 Fwd. 1½ Som. 2 Twists	— — — —	— — — 2.5
— — — —	— — — 2.9	5136 Fwd. 1½ Som. 3 Twists	— — — —	— — — 2.9
— — — —	— — — 2.8	5152 Fwd. 2½ Som. 1 Twist	— — — —	— — — 2.9
— — — —	— — — —	5154 Fwd. 2½ Som. 2 Twists	— — — —	— — — —
1.6 2.0 — —	1.6 1.9 — —	5211 Back Dive, ½ Twist	1.6 — — —	1.7 — — —
2.1 — — —	2.0 — — —	5212 Back Dive, 1 Twist	— — — —	— — — —
— — 1.7 —	1.8 1.8 — —	5221 Back Som. ½ Twist	— — — —	— — — —
— — 1.9 —	— — — 2.0	5222 Back Som. 1 Twist	— — — —	— — — —
— — 2.1 —	— — — 2.1	5223 Back Som. 1½ Twist	— — — —	— — — —
— — 2.1 —	— — — 2.1	5231 Back 1½ Som. ½ Twist	— — 1.8 —	— — — 2.0
— — 2.6 —	— — — 2.4	5233 Back 1½ Som. 1½ Twist	— — 2.6 —	— — — 2.4
— — 2.8 —	— — — 2.7	5235 Back 1½ Som. 2½ Twists	— — — —	— — — 2.7
1.8 2.2 — —	2.0 2.2 — —	5311 Reverse Dive, ½ Twist	1.7 — — —	1.9 — — —
2.2 — — —	2.2 — — —	5312 Reverse Dive, 1 Twist	— — — —	— — — —
— — 1.8 —	— — 2.0 —	5321 Reverse Som. ½ Twist	— — 1.9 —	— — 2.2 —
— — 2.0 —	— — 2.2 —	5322 Reverse Som. 1 Twist	— — — —	— — — —
— — 2.2 —	— — 2.2 —	5323 Reverse Som. 1½ Twist	— — — —	— — — —
— — 2.2 —	— — 2.2 —	5331 Reverse 1½ Som. ½ Twist	— — — —	— — — 2.3
— — 2.7 —	— — 2.5 —	5333 Reverse 1½ Som. 1½ Twist	— — — —	— — — 2.5
— — 2.9 —	— — 2.8 —	5335 Reverse 1½ Som. 2½ Tw.	— — — —	— — — 2.8
2.0 1.7 — —	2.0 1.8 — —	5411 Inward Dive, ½ Twist	1.8 1.7 — —	2.0 1.9 — —
— — — —	2.2 2.2 — —	5412 Inward Dive, 1 Twist	2.0 1.9 — —	2.1 2.0 — —
1.9 1.9 — —	2.0 2.0 — —	5421 Inward Som. ½ Twist	— — — —	— — — —
— — 2.2 —	— — — —	5422 Inward Som. 1 Twist	— — — —	— — — —
— — — 2.6	— — — —	5432 Inward 1½ Som. 1 Twist	— — — —	— — — 2.4
— — — —	— — — —	5434 Inward 1½ Som. 2 Twists	— — — —	— — — 2.8
		VI · ARMSTAND DIVES		
— — — —	— — — —	610 Armstand Dive	1.3 — — —	1.4 — — —
— — — —	— — — —	611 Armstand, back fall	1.4 — — —	1.9 — — —
— — — —	— — — —	612 Armstand somersault	1.6 1.5 1.4 —	1.7 1.6 1.5 —
— — — —	— — — —	614 Armstand Double Som.	— 2.1 — —	— 2.3 2.2 —
— — — —	— — — —	631 Armstand, fwd. cut-thru	— 1.4 1.3 —	1.7 1.6 1.5 —
— — — —	— — — —	632 Armstand, cut-thru, rev. dive	— 2.0 — —	— 2.3 2.1 —
— — — —	— — — —	633 Armstand cut-thru rev. som.	— 1.8 — —	— 1.9 — —

DIVING SCORE FORM

Order of Diving

Must be filed before:

PLACE

Name:	Meet:					
Affiliation or Home Address:	City:		M	W	1-M	3-M	Plat
City:	State:	Date:	State	PRE LIM	SEM FIN	FIN
		Time		POINTS		

NO.	GROUP, POSITION, EXECUTION	DEG OF DIFF	JUDGES' SCORES	NET TOTAL	A W A R D
			1	2	3	4	5	6	7		
1	FWD BACK REV INW ½TW ARM DIVE ..... SOM ..... TW CUT THRU S R FLY TUCK PIKE LAY FREE				
2	FWD BACK REV INW ½TW ARM DIVE ..... SOM ..... TW CUT THRU S R FLY TUCK PIKE LAY FREE				
3	FWD BACK REV INW ½TW ARM DIVE SOM TW CUT THRU S R FLY TUCK PIKE LAY FREE				
4	FWD BACK REV INW ½TW ARM DIVE SOM ..... TW CUT THRU S R FLY TUCK PIKE LAY FREE				
5	FWD BACK REV INW ½TW ARM DIVE SOM ..... TW CUT THRU S R FLY TUCK PIKE LAY FREE				
6	FWD BACK REV INW ½TW ARM DIVE SOM ..... TW CUT THRU S R FLY TUCK PIKE LAY FREE				
7	FWD BACK REV INW ½TW ARM DIVE .... SOM ..... TW CUT THRU S R FLY TUCK PIKE LAY FREE				
8	FWD BACK REV INW ½TW ARM DIVE SOM ..... TW CUT THRU S R FLY TUCK PIKE LAY FREE				
9	FWD BACK REV INW ½TW ARM DIVE .... SOM TW CUT THRU S R FLY TUCK PIKE LAY FREE				
10	FWD BACK REV INW ½TW ARM DIVE SOM TW CUT THRU S R FLY TUCK PIKE LAY FREE				
11	FWD BACK REV INW ½TW ARM DIVE SOM TW CUT THRU S R FLY TUCK PIKE LAY FREE				

INSTRUCTIONS TO DIVERS:

Encircle group, dive and position. Add number of somersaults and twists where applicable. List correct degree of difficulty, then sign name here.

REFEREE: JUDGES:

1
SEC'Y: 2
          3
CLERKS: 4
          5
          6
Enry fee pd.   7

DIVING SHEET

Before a competition, the diver completes his diving sheet and turns it over to the meet referee. The diving sheet lists the dives in the order of performance for that diver. If certain dives are performed out of order, those dives will be given a zero. Also, if the diver does not complete an attempted dive, he will be given a zero for that dive.

More specific information on rules governing diving competitions may be obtained from the following:

Abbreviation		Rules Governing:
NFSHSA	— National Federation of State High School Associations	High School boys
NAIA	— National Association of Intercollegiate Athletics	College men
DGWS	— Division for Girls' and Women's Sports	College women
AAU	— Amateur Athletic Union	Amateur men and women
USOC	— United States Olympic Committee	Age-group children Olympic trials